COMPACT *Research*

Drug Addiction

Diseases and Disorders

ReferencePoint
Press®

San Diego, CA

Select* books in the Compact Research series include:

Current Issues

Animal Experimentation
Cloning
Conflict in the Middle East
DNA Evidence and
    Investigation
Drugs and Sports
Energy Alternatives
Gangs
Genetic Engineering
Genetic Testing
Global Warming and
    Climate Change
Gun Control

Immigration
Islam
National Security
Nuclear Weapons and
    Security
Obesity
Online Social Networking
Stem Cells
Teen Smoking
Terrorist Attacks
Video Games
World Energy Crisis

Diseases and Disorders

Alzheimer's Disease
Autism
Bipolar Disorders
Epilepsy
HPV
Herpes
Influenza

Obsessive-Compulsive
    Disorder
Post-Traumatic Stress
    Disorder
Self-Injury Disorder
Sexually Transmitted
    Diseases

Drugs

Antidepressants
Club Drugs
Cocaine and Crack
Hallucinogens
Heroin
Inhalants
Marijuana

Methamphetamine
Nicotine and Tobacco
Painkillers
Performance-Enhancing
    Drugs
Prescription Drugs
Steroids

Energy and the Environment

Biofuels
Deforestation
Garbage and Recycling
Hydrogen Power

Nuclear Power
Solar Power
Toxic Waste
Wind Power

*For a complete list of titles please visit www.referencepointpress.com.

Drug Addiction

Leanne K. Currie-McGhee

Diseases and Disorders

ReferencePoint
Press®

San Diego, CA

ReferencePoint Press®

For more information, contact:
ReferencePoint Press, Inc.
PO Box 27779
San Diego, CA 92198
www.ReferencePointPress.com

Picture credits:
Cover: iStockphoto.com
Maury Aaseng: 32–34, 46–48, 60–62, 74–76
AP Images: 11
Science Photo Library: 16

LIBRARY OF CONGRESS CATALOGING-IN-PUBLICATION DATA

Currie-McGhee, L. K. (Leanne K.)
  Drug addiction / by Leanne Currie-McGhee.
    p. cm. — (Compact research series. Current issues)
  Includes bibliographical references and index.
  ISBN-13: 978-1-60152-109-5 (hardback)
  ISBN-10: 1-60152-109-X (hardback)
  1. Drug addiction—Juvenile literature. I. Title.
  HV5809.5.C87   2010
  613.8—dc22
                                                                2009045174

Contents

Foreword

❝Where is the knowledge we have lost in information?❞

—T.S. Eliot, "The Rock."

As modern civilization continues to evolve, its ability to create, store, distribute, and access information expands exponentially. The explosion of information from all media continues to increase at a phenomenal rate. By 2020 some experts predict the worldwide information base will double every 73 days. While access to diverse sources of information and perspectives is paramount to any democratic society, information alone cannot help people gain knowledge and understanding. Information must be organized and presented clearly and succinctly in order to be understood. The challenge in the digital age becomes not the creation of information, but how best to sort, organize, enhance, and present information.

ReferencePoint Press developed the *Compact Research* series with this challenge of the information age in mind. More than any other subject area today, researching current issues can yield vast, diverse, and unqualified information that can be intimidating and overwhelming for even the most advanced and motivated researcher. The *Compact Research* series offers a compact, relevant, intelligent, and conveniently organized collection of information covering a variety of current topics ranging from illegal immigration and deforestation to diseases such as anorexia and meningitis.

The series focuses on three types of information: objective single-author narratives, opinion-based primary source quotations, and facts and statistics. The clearly written objective narratives provide context and reliable background information. Primary source quotes are carefully selected and cited, exposing the reader to differing points of view. And facts and statistics sections aid the reader in evaluating perspectives. Presenting these key types of information creates a richer, more balanced learning experience.

For better understanding and convenience, the series enhances information by organizing it into narrower topics and adding design features that make it easy for a reader to identify desired content. For example, in *Compact Research: Illegal Immigration*, a chapter covering the economic impact of illegal immigration has an objective narrative explaining the various ways the economy is impacted, a balanced section of numerous primary source quotes on the topic, followed by facts and full-color illustrations to encourage evaluation of contrasting perspectives.

The ancient Roman philosopher Lucius Annaeus Seneca wrote, "It is quality rather than quantity that matters." More than just a collection of content, the *Compact Research* series is simply committed to creating, finding, organizing, and presenting the most relevant and appropriate amount of information on a current topic in a user-friendly style that invites, intrigues, and fosters understanding.

Drug Addiction at a Glance

Who Is Affected

Studies show that approximately 23 million Americans are addicted to drugs or alcohol.

Brain Disease

Some experts consider drug addiction a brain disease because drugs change the way the brain communicates with the body. Excessive drug use can cause the brain to tell the body it needs drugs to survive.

Teenage Use

In 2008, based on respondents' answers to the annual National Survey on Drug Use and Health, an estimated 1.9 million youths aged 12 to 17 in the United States were classified as needing treatment for substance abuse or addiction.

Drug-Addicted Criminals

Drug abuse and addiction among prison inmates is more than four times that of the general population.

Physical Problems

Drug and alcohol addiction can lead to liver disease, lung cancer, and stroke—all of which can be fatal.

Prevention

Studies have shown that prevention programs that teach children about the problems of drug addiction help reduce the chances of them becoming addicted to or abusing drugs and alcohol.

Treatment

In 2008, 4 million persons in the United Statement received treatment for a problem related to the use of alcohol or illicit drugs. The most common treatment programs are self-help groups such as Alcoholics Anonymous and Narcotics Anonymous.

Vaccines

Scientists are currently developing vaccines that are designed to help substance addicts stop using drugs or help prevent recovered addicts from relapsing.

Overview

❝Alcohol and drugs are not the problems; they are what people are using to help themselves cope with the problems. Those problems always have both physical and psychological components.❞

—Chris Prentiss, author of *The Alcoholism and Addiction Cure*.

❝Every single addict can be helped, no matter how far gone they seem to be, no matter how seemingly determined they are to hurt or even to kill themselves.❞

—Morteza Khaleghi, author of *Free from Addiction*.

What Is Drug Addiction?

Drugs are substances of natural or synthetic origin that can alter a person's emotional or physical state. Drugs are often used to treat or prevent diseases, relieve pains, help control mental or physical ailments, and even to help diagnose illnesses. However, some people try drugs for other reasons, such as wanting to experience a changed emotional or physical state.

Any person who uses drugs has a chance of becoming addicted to drugs. Drug addiction occurs when a person takes increasing amounts of drugs, to the point that drug use becomes the center of his or her life. The National Institutes of Health defines drug addiction as an uncontrollable compulsion to seek and use drugs, even in the face of negative health and social consequences. This means a drug addict will go to great

A pouch containing crystal meth is displayed beside a homemade pipe. Crystal meth is a very pure, smokeable form of methamphetamine. It is a powerful and extremely addictive man-made stimulant; its use can lead to severe physiological and psychological dependence.

lengths, risking physical health, personal relationships, and job or school performance, in order to get drugs.

At 18 years old, Michael Reichman risked everything because of his substance addiction. He had just moved to Atlanta and was looking for fun. He started taking methamphetamine (also called meth) with friends and quickly became addicted. Reichman writes:

> My mother came down to check on me and I was living in filth. There was trash all over the counters, the floor, my bed. Paranoia had set in. I stayed in the far corner of my room, on the far corner of a mattress that was so filthy my parents threw it out when they came down. Most of

my clothes were missing. I sold everything of value, my money was half gone. I never bothered to get a job. I moved onto the streets.[1]

Reichman got treatment and stopped using methamphetamine for two years but then relapsed. He continues to struggle with his addiction and admits that he still is not sure he is free from the lure of drugs.

Misconceptions About Prescription Drugs

In the past few years, addiction to prescription drugs has become an increasing problem. This is because people hold the misconception that it is safe to take these drugs because they are legal if obtained from a doctor. However, if people take prescription drugs without a prescription or do not follow the doctor's directions, they are abusing the drugs. As with any drug, people who take more and more of a prescription drug have probably developed an addiction.

Addiction to prescription drugs such as painkillers is rising. In 2008, 1.7 million people in the United States were addicted to or abusing pain relievers, compared with 1.5 million in 2002. Addiction to and abuse of prescription drugs has become so prevalent that in some areas prescription drug abuse is starting to outpace illegal drug use. A Florida Medical Examiners Commission analysis of autopsies in 2007 found that the rate of deaths caused by prescription drugs was three times the rate of deaths caused by all illicit drugs combined.

Drugs Commonly Associated with Addiction

One of the most common substances that people are addicted to is nicotine. In 2008, according to the U.S. Department of Health and Human Services National Survey on Drug Use and Health, an estimated 70.9 million Americans aged 12 or older were current users of a tobacco product. The majority of these were current cigarette smokers, with 59.8 million persons. Of these, reports the American Council on Science and Health, 70 percent want to quit, and 40 percent actually make a serious attempt to quit each year. However, each year fewer than 5 percent actually succeed in quitting permanently.

The 2008 survey also determined the number of people in the United States who received treatment for drug and alcohol addiction or abuse.

Information was gathered from from civilian, noninstitutionalized people 12 years of age or older in all 50 states and the District of Columbia. According to the survey, more people received treatment for alcohol addiction and abuse than for any other substance. An estimated 1.6 million people in the United States received treatment for problems with alcohol in 2008. Significant numbers of people also received treatment for marijuana addiction; in 2008 that number totaled 947,000. That same year, the survey found, approximately 336,000 people in the United States received help for addiction to stimulants such as cocaine and methamphetamine.

> " Any person who uses drugs has a chance of becoming addicted to drugs. "

Addiction to prescription drugs such as painkillers and tranquilizers has become a big problem in the past decade. In 2008 more than 600,000 people in the United States received treatment for addiction to painkillers, and more than 300,000 were treated for tranquilizer addiction. Actor Burt Reynolds admitted to being treated for addiction to prescription drugs in 2009. "I felt that in spite of the fact I am supposedly a big tough guy, I couldn't beat prescription drugs on my own," Reynolds said of his addiction. "I've worked hard to get off of them and really hope other people will realize they need to seek professional help, rather than ignoring the problem or trying to get off of the prescriptions on their own."[2]

What Causes Drug Addiction?

Approximately 10 percent of all people who experiment with drugs become addicted, according to the University of Utah's Genetic Science Learning Center. If a person starts taking drugs and takes them in increasing amounts over time, experts would likely classify that person as a drug abuser. Some drug abusers are able to stop taking drugs when needed, such as when they need to go to work or attend to their personal lives, but others cannot stop their drug use. Those who cannot stop their drug use, even when they have important work or personal matters to take care of, are considered addicts.

People can become addicted to drugs because of the physical changes drugs produce in the body. Drugs are chemicals that tap into the brain's communication system and disrupt the way brain cells normally send, receive, and process information. Because of this disruption, the brain perceives that it "needs" the drug, so addicts begin to feel they cannot live without the drug. Also, with continued use of the drug, the body's ability to produce certain chemicals is diminished because the drug replaces the chemicals. As a result, the person's body then needs the drug to function and demands the drug through physical cravings.

Drug cravings often become so severe that the addict will do almost anything to get more of the drug. "At first, people may perceive what seem to be positive effects with drug use," reports the National Institute on Drug Abuse (NIDA). "They also may believe that they can control their use; however, drugs can quickly take over their lives."[3]

Disease Versus Behavior

There is debate about whether drug addiction is a disease or a behavioral problem. Some doctors believe that although drug use begins as a voluntary choice, after time addicted people cannot stop their behavior because the drugs have changed how their brains work. "Today, scientists and physicians overwhelmingly agree that while use and even abuse of drugs such as alcohol and cocaine is a behavior over which the individual exerts control, addiction to these substances is something different," writes health writer Janet Firshein.[4] These doctors view addiction as a disease of the brain and, as such, it can only be cured with professional help such as medical intervention.

> There is debate about whether drug addiction is a disease or a behavioral problem.

Other medical professionals disagree. Although physical cravings are a fact of drug addiction, these experts believe that people have the power to overcome those cravings. They have to be willing to learn behaviors that will help them resist the desire for the drugs. "Addiction is not as hopeless or uncontrollable as the brain disease metaphor suggests," write Sally Satel and Scott Lilienfeld, a psychiatrist and psychologist who specialize in drug addiction. "Yes, like other bad habits, it is in our brains— but like other bad habits, it can be broken."[5] They point to the fact that most recovered addicts attribute their recovery to personal choices.

Addictive Qualities of Drugs

Not all drugs have the same addictive qualities. Some drugs are more addictive than others because they create physical addiction, which is when a person's body physically craves the drugs and reacts negatively when not getting the drugs. These types of drugs, such as heroin or methamphetamine, can also cause serious physical damage to the addict and, because of this and their addictive qualities, are considered "hard" drugs.

Researchers at the NIDA and the University of California at San Francisco ranked the addictiveness of various drugs based on severity of withdrawal symptoms and physical problems that arise once an addict stops taking drugs, among other factors. Using these and other criteria, heroin and cocaine were ranked among the most addictive drugs.

Other drugs are less physically addictive than "hard" drugs but can still result in a physical addiction. Additionally, these drugs can be psychologically addictive, which is when a person cannot get by emotionally without taking the drugs. These drugs are referred to as "soft" drugs, and examples include marijuana and Ecstasy. According to the 2008 National Survey on Drug Use and Health, marijuana was the illicit drug with the highest rate of dependence or abuse, with an estimated 4.2 million reported addicts or abusers in the United States. More people try marijuana than any other illicit drug. Of all the people who tried drugs for the first time in 2008, 56.6 percent chose marijuana, more than 30 percent more than any other drug choice. This results in an increased pool of people who risk becoming addicted. Marijuana dependence proves that any drug, whether hard or soft, can result in addiction.

> " One of the most dangerous aspects of drug addiction is that it can kill a person. "

What Are the Dangers of Drug Addiction?

One of the most dangerous aspects of drug addiction is that it can kill a person. Every year, abuse of drugs and alcohol contributes to the deaths of more than 100,000 Americans due to both physical problems, such as lung cancer caused by smoking, and accidents that are drug and alcohol-related. Approximately 10 to 20 percent of alcoholics develop the

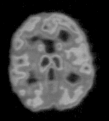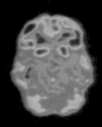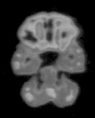

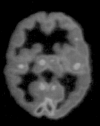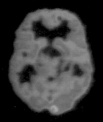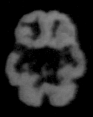

BRAIN METABOLISM

NORMAL SUBJECT

COCAINE ABUSER
LATE DETOXIFICATION

BNL PET STUDY

Even after four months of abstinence, the brain of a heavy cocaine user shows less activity than the brain of a nonuser. The colored scans at the top show horizontal sections of a normal, or nonuser's, brain. The scans at the bottom show sections of a brain four months after heavy cocaine use. The front of the brains are at the top of each scan, and the slices get deeper from left to right. The brighter, yellow areas of the brain are those of high activity. The brain of the cocaine user is shown to be much less active than the brain of the nonuser.

potentially-fatal condition cirrhosis, or scarring, of the liver as a result of excessive and chronic alcohol use. Additionally, tobacco is linked to an estimated 440,000 deaths per year in the United States due to addiction to cigarettes and other tobacco products.

Drug and alcohol addiction can also result in accidents caused by impaired driving that may kill the addicts and others. Approximately 41 percent of all motor vehicle accidents are alcohol related, and alcoholics, due to their excessive and frequent drinking, run a higher risk of being involved in these types of accidents.

Mental health issues are another problem associated with drug addiction. According to the NIDA, between 30 and 60 percent of drug abusers, many of them addicts, have concurrent mental health issues, and doctors believe that drug use may exacerbate the mental problems. Also, substance addiction can lead to suicide as the lifetime risk for suicide death among alcohol-dependent individuals has been estimated to be 7 to 10 percent, according to the Department of Health and Human Services. Personal problems also result from drug addiction as drug addicts often become so focused on obtaining drugs that they lose their jobs, home, family, and friends in pursuit of the drugs.

The Most Dangerous Drugs

Although all drug addiction is dangerous, some drugs have a greater negative impact on people's lives and on society than others. In a 2007 study published in the medical journal *Lancet*, psychiatrists and police officers evaluated 20 different drugs. Of these drugs, they rated the following as the top 10 most dangerous drugs: heroin, cocaine, barbiturates, street methadone, alcohol, ketamine (a hallucinogen), benzodiazepines (types of sedatives), amphetamines, tobacco, and buprenorphine (an addictive opioid that is used in the treatment of heroin addiction).

> **Drug addiction can be prevented if people are convinced early on not to experiment with or try drugs.**

One criterion for this list was the physical harm the drugs do to the user, which is why heroin ranks at the top. Heroin can lead to pneumonia, resistance to infections, and bacterial infections of blood vessels and heart valves, and those who take it intravenously increase their physical danger. Intravenous drugs can cause the spread of infectious diseases such as HIV and hepatitis B and carry a high risk of causing sudden death from respiratory depression, which is shallow breathing that can result in a lack of oxygen in the blood.

Another factor in the study was how the drugs impact society, such as which drugs are associated with the most accidents and police intervention. Alcohol and tobacco cause 40 percent of all hospital illnesses. Additionally, alcohol is involved in more than 50 percent of all visits to hospital emergency rooms.

Prevention of Drug Addiction

Studies have shown that drug addiction can be prevented if people are convinced early on not to experiment with or try drugs. The Partnership for a Drug-Free America states that young people are less likely to try drugs when parents discuss the consequences of drug use from an early age. According to the Partnership for a Drug-Free America, when kids understand that drugs are harmful, this knowledge will keep them from trying them. Additionally, even if kids have already started using drugs, prevention programs have been found to reduce their drug use. Overall, these programs significantly reduce the chance of young people becoming addicts. The key is to communicate effectively the severe problems that can result from drug abuse and addiction in order to make an impact on kids.

The NIDA has studied prevention programs used at schools and by communities and found that young people who participated in these programs were less likely to use drugs than those who were not in the programs. One of the programs, Project ALERT, reaches more than 1.5 million middle school students in all 50 states each year. This 2-year program focuses on preventing the use of alcohol, tobacco, marijuana, and inhalants by having students act out situations involving drug use, its consequences, and how to deal with pressure to use drugs. The program is taught in the classroom with role-playing activities, videos, and homework assignments that involve parents. One study showed that Project ALERT has prevented or reduced cigarette and marijuana use among eighth-grade students. Specifically, one study found that the program

> " Drug addiction is not easily overcome, but it is a treatable affliction. "

kept 40 percent of the early cigarette experimenters from becoming regular smokers, and another study found that Project ALERT participants were nearly 50 percent less likely than nonparticipants to have become marijuana users by eighth grade. The belief is that by eliminating or even reducing drug use among youth, the risk of addiction will also decrease.

Can Drug Addiction Be Overcome?

Drug addiction is not easily overcome, but it is a treatable affliction. Alcoholics Anonymous and Narcotics Anonymous are two of the best-known treatment programs. They teach people how to recognize what triggers their drug use and how to respond so that they do not turn to drugs or alcohol.

One population that has benefited from drug treatment is the nation's prison population. Drug abuse or addiction rates of offenders are more than 4 times that of the general population. For this reason many prisons offer drug treatment services. According to a 2006 Bureau of Justice Statistics report, 14.8 percent of state prisoners and 17.4 percent of federal prisoners reported having received drug treatment while incarcerated.

Studies have shown that effective drug treatment during incarceration reduces the likelihood of drug use and drug-related criminal behavior once inmates are released from prison. NIDA director Nora D. Volkow explains:

> Treating drug-abusing offenders improves public health and safety. In addition to the devastating social consequences for individuals and their families, drug abuse exacts serious health effects, including increased risk for infectious diseases such as HIV and hepatitis C; and treatment for addiction can help prevent their spread. Providing drug abusers with treatment also makes it less likely that these abusers will return to the criminal justice system.[6]

In a Delaware Work Release study sponsored by NIDA, prisoners who participated in prison-based drug treatment followed by aftercare were 7 times more likely to be drug free after 3 years than those who did not receive treatment. Nearly 70 percent of those prisoners in the comprehensive drug treatment group remained arrest free after 3 years, compared with only 30 percent in the group that did not get treatment.

Always an Addict

Even when an addict has gone through treatment and gotten clean and sober, the fight is not over. Relapse is always a possibility, and for that reason most addiction professionals agree that aftercare is essential. Aftercare can mean going to meetings, such as Alcoholics Anonymous or Narcotics Anonymous, or going to any other facilitated sessions that teach people how to deal with everyday problems without going back to drugs or alcohol.

Patrick Meninga, an addict of marijuana and alcohol for more than five years, attended two treatment centers to get clean but did not take part in the suggested aftercare programs. Each time he left the treatment center, Meninga relapsed; he finally realized that he could not remain sober on his own. "The length of time you will spend in a residential treatment program is a drop in the bucket, and you should not expect to live 'happily ever after' without some serious follow up to your stay in drug rehab," writes Meninga. "Recovery is a life long process."[7] After Meninga's third time in treatment, he decided to follow the program's advice and participated in an aftercare program.

Eleven years later Meninga remains sober but admits that his fight against addiction will never be over. Addiction is a lifelong disease, and in order to stay in recovery, addicts continually have to fight their urges to avoid falling back into a dangerous lifestyle.

What Is Drug Addiction?

❝All sorts of people can become addicted to drugs from all walks of life—young and old, rich and poor, males and females.❞

—Timothy Fong, physician and consultant to the National Youth Anti-Drug Media Campaign.

❝Abuse and addiction are two very different types of behavior. Abuse defines drug and alcohol use on a social level and even though addiction often begins as such, the disease takes hold of the addict and progresses them to a level where they cannot stop using drugs and alcohol, even if they want to and stand to lose everything.❞

—Oasis Counseling Center, a treatment center for drug addiction.

Drugs Take Control

Addiction begins in different ways. Some people are prescribed drugs to help them sleep or deal with pain, whereas others start smoking cigarettes or drinking alcohol as something to do when they socialize. Still others have friends who pressure them into trying illegal drugs at parties or in other social settings. In these situations people do not take drugs with the intention of becoming addicted; however, in all of these situations, addiction is a possibility. Though some drugs are more addictive than others, 10 to 30 percent of people who use drugs develop an addiction to them.

Whether or not a person becomes addicted may depend on the person's physical, social, and emotional states. Physically, a person's body may become addicted to the drug in that the body craves it when not using, pushing the person to keep doing the drug. Emotionally, people may discover that drugs or alcohol are a way to deal with stress and may use them any time they feel upset in order to deal with their feelings. In social situations people may take drugs to relax or because of peer pressure. All of these situations may lead people to take larger amounts of drugs, resulting in abuse.

> Abuse turns into addiction when people crave the drug to the point that they cannot get through the day without it.

Abuse turns into addiction when people crave the drug to the point that they cannot get through the day without it, even when they know that use will negatively impact their lives. Mindy McConnell started taking drugs as a teenager because she was curious about them. By age 15, her experimentation resulted in a methamphetamine addiction. McConnell writes:

> That one line of meth started me on a path of getting high at school and then eventually dropping out all together. Classes interfered with my drug life. What I thought was normal behavior was not normal at all. I was 17, out of control, addicted to drugs and in the [midst] of all of this, I became pregnant with my son, Isaiah. . . . All I wanted to do was hang out and get high—and I could never get high enough. Sometimes I would be up for days, smoking constantly.[8]

McConnell never planned on being an addict, but drugs took control of her life.

Three Stages of Drug Addiction

According to the Canyon, a drug treatment center in Malibu, California, there are three stages of drug addiction. The first stage is preoccupation/anticipation, which is when people develop an overwhelming urge to use drugs. The drug use preoccupies users and keeps them from putting other events, responsibilities, or relationships first. Signs of this stage are irritability, agitation, and difficulty concentrating. At this point users are abusing the drugs but still may be able to function in everyday life.

The second stage is binge/intoxication. During this stage the user takes increasingly larger amounts of drugs in order to feel an effect. This increasing use leads to bingeing, which can result in an extremely danger-ous level of intoxication, or being high. The warning signs of this stage include missing days at work or school because the user is recovering from a drug or alcohol binge. During this stage the abuse has become addiction, with drugs becoming central to the user's life.

The third stage of addiction is withdrawal/negative effect, which is when the user experiences symptoms such as night terrors, panic attacks, sweating, and anxiety. These symptoms occur as the body tries to rid it-self of the drug while at the same time craving it. By this stage the person is severely addicted and cannot get through the day without drugs.

Misconceptions Lead to Addiction

Some people begin their path to drug addiction because of the miscon-ception that certain drugs are not as harmful or addictive as others. For example, people may consider using marijuana harmless because it is not as physically addictive as harder drugs. However, studies show that many people become addicted to marijuana because they develop a psychologi-cal dependence on it. The need for mari-juana can overcome all of a person's needs and result in disrupting his or her life, just as an addiction to harder drugs can do. "I would come home from work, close my door, have my bong, my food, my music and my dog, and I wouldn't see another person until I went to work the next day,"[9] says Joyce, a marijuana addict who checked herself into a treatment center in 2009.

> Teenagers are particularly vulnerable to prescription addiction.

Prescription drugs are another type of drug that people may consider safe to take because a doctor prescribes them. However, these drugs can be just as addictive and physically harmful as illegal drugs if they are taken without a prescription or if a person takes more than the prescription instructs. The two kinds of prescription drugs that people most commonly become addicted to are opioids and benzodiazepines. Opioids such as morphine, codeine, and oxycodone are used to control pain, while benzodiazepines such as Valium and Xanax are used to manage anxiety. People start taking these drugs to deal with health issues, but if they up their dosage without medical supervision, they increase their chances of becoming addicted.

> "Multiple addictions make treatment more difficult because the addict must undergo withdrawal from more than one substance."

Teenagers are particularly vulnerable to prescription addiction because of the misconception that they are safe and because these drugs are easier to obtain than illegal drugs. According to the Mayo Clinic: "Most prescriptions are written for people who have a true medical need for these drugs. But many households have a drawer filled with old prescription bottles containing leftover drugs. Because prescription drugs have medical uses, teens often believe they are a safe alternative to street drugs."[10] The National Institute on Drug Abuse reported that in 2008, 15.4 percent of twelfth graders reported using a prescription drug nonmedically within the past year. Additionally, in 2006 the Substance Abuse and Mental Health Services Administration reported that 15.9 percent of 12- to 17-year-olds had become addicted to or abused prescription drugs in the past year.

The Physical Symptoms of Addiction

People addicted to drugs often experience physical symptoms from the drugs. These include, but are not limited to, frequent exhaustion, weakness, unexplained injuries and infections, blackouts, flashbacks, delusions, and paranoia. Addicts who try to stop using drugs often experience withdrawal symptoms such as nausea, tremors, and sweating.

The specific physical symptoms depend on which drug the person is addicted to. A person who is addicted to a drug that is snorted through the nose, such as cocaine, may have chronic sinusitis or nosebleeds. An addict who smokes marijuana or crack, a concentrated form of cocaine, may have a persistent cough, bronchitis, and frequent bouts of coughing up excessive mucus or blood. People addicted to stimulants such as co-caine and methamphetamine may experience cycles of increased energy, restlessness, and inability to sleep. Opioids, such as heroin, cause addicts to experience confusion and disorientation.

Changes in Behavior

Odd behavior can signal to friends and family that someone close to them is addicted by the person's odd behavior. According to the Mayo Clinic, drug addicts often do things they would not normally do, such as stealing or skipping work. Other symptoms include the inability to handle a stressful situation without resorting to drugs or failing in at-tempts to stop using drugs even though the person wants to stop. Ad-ditional signs of drug addiction include angry outbursts, mood swings, irritability, manic behavior, talking incoherently, and risky, secretive, and suspicious behavior.

One specific behavior associated with addiction is doing whatever is necessary to get the money to pay for the drug. People addicted to crack spend at least $200 a day for the drug, and heroin addicts spend about $150 a day, says Ken-neth Martin, program director at McKenna House in Washington D.C., a homeless shelter that deals with many drug addicts.

> **Most professionals consider drug and alcohol addiction a chronic disease.**

Many addicts end up stealing, even from family and friends, to pay for their drugs. Dawn realized the full extent of her addiction to prescription drugs when her mother caught her stealing. Dawn writes:

> I lived to use and used to live. I sat at home using in de-nial until my mother called on October 30, 2005. She was yelling and telling me to stay away from her because she just got her bank statement from my dad's trust fund. She asked why I stole that much money, and then she asked if I was doing drugs. Something was different this time, and I cried out, "Yes, mom, I'm on drugs and it's bad."[11]

This behavior made Dawn realize how serious her addiction had gotten, and she sought treatment, becoming sober in 2005 and having remained so since.

Multiple Addictions and Cross-Addiction

People with multiple addictions are those who are addicted to more than one substance at the same time. Addiction to tobacco and alcohol or drugs is quite common; the smoking rate among chemically dependent people is estimated to be as high as 90 percent. According to the 2008 National Survey on Drug Use and Health, among the 17.3 million heavy drinkers aged 12 or older, 29.4 percent also use illicit drugs. Additionally, the survey found that 3.1 million people are estimated to be dependent on or abusing both alcohol and illicit drugs.

Multiple addictions make treatment more difficult because the addict must undergo withdrawal from more than one substance. Additionally, with multiple addictions there are often more social and emotional triggers that cause the drug or alcohol use than with addiction to only one substance. This means the addict must really learn to understand triggers and to change his or her behavior in order to conquer the addiction.

Cross-addiction also involves the use of more than one drug. However, with cross-addiction an addict changes from one drug to another. For example, if the addict stops using cocaine but starts using alcohol recreationally, the addict will become addicted to alcohol. Being cross-addicted means that the person will become addicted to any substance he or she tries. According to Sarah Senghas, who works in a substance abuse treatment facility, cross-addiction means that addicts can and will become addicted to any mind- or mood-altering substance, even if it was not their original drug of choice. "Alcohol? Cocaine? Hydrocodone? There are many drugs of choice, but no matter the substance, if you are addicted to one, you are addicted to it all,"[12] writes Senghas.

Lifelong Affliction?

Most professionals consider drug and alcohol addiction a chronic disease, meaning it is a lifelong condition that must always be treated. This means that once a person becomes addicted to drugs or alcohol, the person can never go back to taking them recreationally without becoming dependent on them. "Drug addiction is a lifelong problem. It is treatable but there is no cure to it,"[13] said Renato De Los Reyes, a practicing psychiatrist in Illinois.

Not everyone agrees with this assessment. There is a school of thought that says that alcoholism and drug addiction are on a continuum, with some people so severely addicted to drugs or alcohol that abstinence is the only answer, whereas other people may have more treatable addictions and can take an occasional drink without relapsing. "To say if you are alcoholic you must never drink again is over-simplified—alcohol dependence is on a continuum,"[14] says Nick Heather, a professor of alcohol and other drug studies in the Division of Psychology at Northumbria University. Heather believes that some addicts can learn to control their drinking to the point that one glass of wine or beer will not lead to bingeing or a relapse.

Whether a recovered addict can have an occasional drink or try a drug without relapsing continues to be debated, but what is not debated is that addiction is a serious problem. Over 23 million people in the United States use drugs or alcohol to the point that they are considered addicted and in need of treatment. The addiction problem has resulted in numerous health, social, and personal problems in the lives of addicts, their friends and families, and the communities in which they live.

What Is Drug Addiction?

❝Directly or indirectly, every community is affected by drug abuse and addiction, as is every family. Drugs take a tremendous toll on our society at many levels.❞

—National Institute on Drug Abuse, "Magnitude," January 2, 2008. www.nida.nih.gov.

The National Institute on Drug Abuse is part of the U.S. government's National Institutes of Health, with a mission to use science to understand and fight drug abuse and addiction.

❝Addicts come from broken and intact homes. They are longtime losers and great successes. We often heard in lectures or Al-Anon meetings or AA meetings of the bright and charming men and women who bewilder those around them when they wind up in the gutter.❞

—David Sheff, *Beautiful Boy*. New York: Houghton Mifflin, 2008.

Sheff is the father of Nic Sheff, who struggles with drug addiction and has written his own book about this experience.

* Editor's Note: While the definition of a primary source can be narrowly or broadly defined, for the purposes of Compact Research, a primary source consists of: 1) results of original research presented by an organization or researcher; 2) eyewitness accounts of events, personal experience, or work experience; 3) first-person editorials offering pundits' opinions; 4) government officials presenting political plans and/or policies; 5) representatives of organizations presenting testimony or policy.

❝I was constantly insecure and terrified and thinking there was something wrong with me. Doing drugs was the only thing that could relieve me of that constant stream of self loathing circulating through my mind.❞

—Nic Sheff, quoted in BookReporter, "Author Talk," May 2, 2008. www.bookreporter.com.

Sheff is the son of David Sheff, who wrote *Beautiful Boy* about dealing with his son's drug addiction. Sheff has also written about his drug addiction in *Tweak*, his autobiography.

....

❝For most people, no, marijuana is not addictive. The vast majority of pot smokers never become addicted.❞

—Buddy T., "Is Marijuana Really Addictive?" About.com, April 16, 2009. http://alcoholism.about.com.

Buddy T. writes the Alcoholism Guide for About.com and also writes on other substance abuse and addiction subjects.

....

❝For some, marijuana can be highly addictive. Researchers estimate that approximately 10–14% of marijuana users develop serious dependency.❞

—Drug Addiction Treatment, "Is Marijuana Addictive?" May 8, 2009. www.drugaddictiontreatment.com.

Drug Addiction Treatment is a Web site devoted to providing up-to-date information and resources related to drug addiction and the most effective treatment options.

....

❝Substance addiction tends not to be confined to a particular mood altering drug. . . . When you have one addiction, you get the whole set thrown in for free—even before you have experienced the other drugs.**❞**

—Michael Bloch, "Cross Addiction," World Wide Addiction, 2007. www.worldwideaddiction.com.

Bloch is a recovered alcoholic and drug addict who has experienced cross-addiction.

....

❝I know from my own experience that continuing to smoke while recovering from alcoholism seemed to give me a welcome substitute to fall back upon when I really wanted a drink. I found over time, though, that I was using it as a crutch to avoid my feelings. It wasn't until I was free of cigarettes too that I felt I could really start to develop as a whole and sober person.**❞**

—Anne Mitchell, "Smoking and Alcoholism: How to Fight Multiple Addictions, Part II," COPDConnection, July 22, 2008. www.healthcentral.com.

Mitchell is a recovering alcoholic and former smoker and the author of *Give It Up! Stop Smoking for Life.*

....

Facts and Illustrations

What Is Drug Addiction?

- According to the 2008 National Survey on Drug Use and Health, **15.2 million persons** in the United States aged 12 or older are addicted to or are abusers of alcohol.

- The 2008 National Survey on Drug Use and Health found that **3.9 million people** in the United States are dependent on or abuse illicit drugs.

- The American Psychiatric Association defines someone as drug dependent or addicted if that person exhibits **three or more symptoms of dependence**, such as using larger amounts of a drug over time, inability to stop the drug use, and withdrawal from family and friends.

- A 2009 University of California at San Diego study found that men are **two times more likely** than women to become alcoholics.

- According to the Institute of Medicine of the National Academy of Sciences, **32 percent** of people who try tobacco become dependent, as do **23 percent** of those who try heroin, **17 percent** who try cocaine, **15 percent** who try alcohol, and **9 percent** who try marijuana.

- More than **5 million Americans** were addicted to narcotic pain relievers in 2007, an increase of 800,000 from 2004, reports the U.S. Drug Enforcement Administration.

Number of U.S. Substance Abusers and Addicts Remains Steady

In 2008, an estimated 22.2 million persons aged 12 or older were classified as substance abusers or addicts. Of these, 3.1 million were classified as addicted to both alcohol and illicit drugs; 3.9 million were addicted to illicit drugs alone; and 15.2 million were addicted to or abusers of alcohol alone. Overall, the number of substance abusers or addicts remained steady between 2002 and 2008.

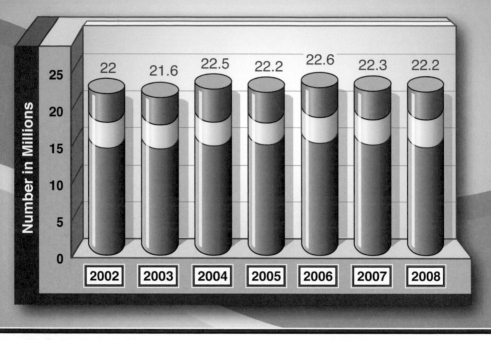

Source: U.S. Department of Health and Human Services, "National Survey on Drug Use and Health," 2008. http://oas.samhsa.gov.

• Nearly **3 out of 10** teens believe prescription pain relievers—even if not prescribed by a doctor—are not addictive, reports the Partnership for a Drug-Free America.

Drugs Most Commonly Used by Twelfth Graders

Seven of the 11 drugs most frequently abused by U.S. high school seniors are prescription and over-the-counter drugs. Marijuana was the most commonly abused drug among these students between 2007 and 2008, but 15.4 percent of twelfth graders reported abusing prescription drugs within that time period.

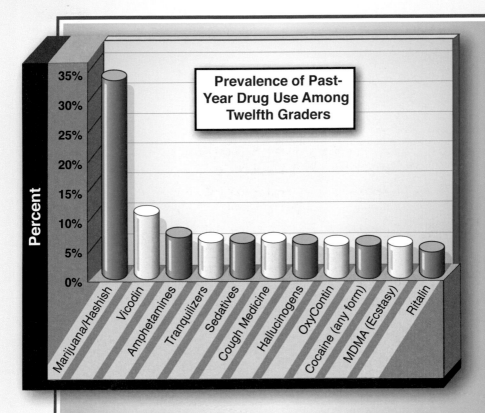

Prevalence of Past-Year Drug Use Among Twelfth Graders

Source: National Institute on Drug Abuse, "Prescription/Over the Counter Drugs Account for 7 of 11 of the Most Frequently Abused Drugs," 2008. www.drugabuse.gov.

- According to the National Institute on Drug Abuse, **35 million** people in the United States attempt to quit using tobacco each year, but more than **85 percent** of those relapse, most within a week, due to nicotine's addictive properties.

Drug Use by Drug Type

In the 2007 National Survey on Drug Use and Health, the U.S. Department of Health and Human Services estimates how many Americans used illicit drugs and which types they used during a one-month period before the survey.

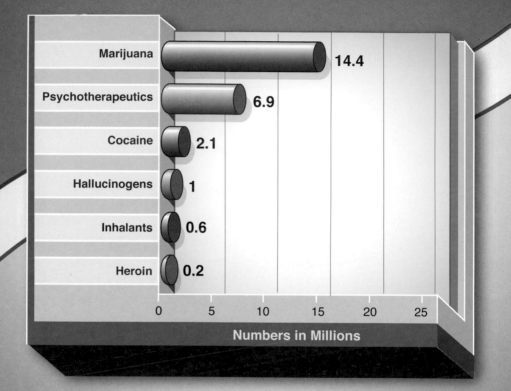

Marijuana 14.4
Psychotherapeutics 6.9
Cocaine 2.1
Hallucinogens 1
Inhalants 0.6
Heroin 0.2

0   5   10   15   20   25

Numbers in Millions

Source: U.S. Department of Health and Human Services, "Results from the 2007 National Survey on Drug Use and Health: National Findings," September 4, 2008. www.drugabusestatistics.samhsa.gov.

- **Four out of 10** teens agree that **prescription medicines** are much safer to use than illegal drugs even if a doctor does not prescribe them, reports the Partnership for a Drug-Free America.

- The *New York Times* reported that the percentage of those seeking treatment for marijuana addiction had increased to **16 percent** in 2007 from **12 percent** in 1997.

What Causes Drug Addiction?

66Some people have a genetic predisposition to addiction. But because it involves these basic brain functions, everyone will become an addict if sufficiently exposed to drugs or alcohol.99

—Nora D. Volkow, director of the National Institute on Drug Abuse.

66The reason why I had needed [alcohol] in the beginning was that I had lost my path in life. When our life feels meaningless then of course we are going to look for ways to ease the pain. When we find our path again we no longer need any addiction to help us manage things.99

—Paul Garrigan, recovered alcoholic, 2009.

Risk of Addiction

Anyone who tries drugs runs the risk of addiction. The likelihood of a drug user becoming addicted depends on many factors, including genetics, physical health, mental health, and age. According to the Institute of Medicine of the National Academy of Sciences, 32 percent of people who try tobacco become dependent, as do 23 percent of those who try heroin. Seventeen percent of people who try cocaine, 15 percent who try alcohol, and 9 percent who try marijuana also become addicted. Whether people initially take drugs for fun, because they are curious, or as a result of peer pressure, they risk becoming addicts.

Evan started taking drugs at age 13. At first the drugs seemed like fun, but soon he discovered that he could not live without them. "Drugs turned me into a bad person," Evan says. "I was lying, stealing, and cheating to get my drugs. My life went downhill fast. At first it was fun, but then it got to where I couldn't get out of bed without heroin."[15]

Who Is at Risk?

Personality, physiology, and daily life experiences can determine whether someone is more or less likely to develop an addiction. For example, a person suffering from low self-esteem is more at risk for becoming dependent on drugs or alcohol than those who have higher self-esteem. According to a 2006 study conducted at Florida State University, 11-year-old boys who displayed evidence of low self-esteem in the sixth or seventh grade were 1.6 times more likely than other children to be addicted to drugs 9 years later.

Research has also shown that people who have experienced extreme or chronic stress have an increased likelihood of developing a drug addiction. This type of stress is known as post-traumatic stress disorder (PTSD). It is commonly seen in members of the military who have returned from war zones, but it also affects people who have experienced traumatic situations such as abuse, violence, and even severe natural disasters. "Drug dependence has frequently been observed in war veterans who also suffer from PTSD," said Andreas Heinz, director and chair of the Department of Psychiatry at Charité University Medical Center Berlin. "Both men and women often increase drug abuse and develop dependence following war and other trauma."[16] A 2009 study by the Department of Psychiatry and Psychotherapy at University Medical Center Hamburg-Eppendorf in Hamburg, Germany, found that from one-third to one-half of those seeking treatment for substance abuse could also have PTSD.

> **Personality, physiology, and daily life experiences can determine whether someone is more or less likely to develop an addiction.**

Another major risk factor for drug addiction is genetics. When a biological family member—a parent or grandparent, for instance—is addicted to drugs, other family members are more susceptible to drug addiction as well. Scientists estimate that genetic factors account for between 40 and 60 percent of a person's vulnerability to addiction. However, doctors stress that genetics does not mean a person will definitely become an addict. "Just because you are prone to addiction doesn't mean you're going to become addicted," says Glen Hanson. "It just means you've got to be careful."[17]

Changes in the Brain

When people start taking drugs, they initially do so by choice, but continual use may take their choice away. Studies have shown that excessive use of drugs can change how the brain communicates with the rest of the body. This may result in a compulsion to keep taking drugs, a factor that overrides the ability to make practical decisions about drug use.

The brain communicates with the rest of the body through neurons and neurotransmitters that tell people how to feel, what to think, and what to do. One important neurotransmitter is dopamine, which is a controlling factor in the brain's reward system. Dopamine is present in regions of the brain that control movement, emotion, motivation, and feelings of pleasure. Activities like eating increase dopamine production, which tells the brain that the activity feels good and should be done again.

Drugs such as heroin, amphetamines, cocaine, alcohol, and nicotine cause the brain to produce increased amounts of dopamine. When drugs result in increased levels of dopamine, people's brains tell them to take the drugs again and again. As a person continues to use these drugs, the brain needs more dopamine to achieve the same pleasure it got when the person first started doing drugs. This compels people to increase the amount of drugs, eventually creating a cycle that leads to addiction.

Gateway Drugs

Many believe recreational drugs such as marijuana are gateway drugs that lead to the use of harder drugs such as heroin or amphetamines. For example, a 2009 Rasmussen poll found that nearly half of all American voters believe marijuana use leads to use of harder drugs. Additionally, the National Center on Addiction and Substance Abuse at Columbia University found that adolescents who smoke marijuana are 85 times more likely to use cocaine than their non-marijuana-smoking peers. When people try harder drugs such as heroin, amphetamines, or cocaine, they increase their chances of becoming drug addicts because these drugs are highly physically addictive.

Others disagree with the idea that marijuana leads to harder drugs and addiction. Opponents of the idea of gateway drugs cite current studies that have found that a person's behavior, not the type of drugs the person tries, leads to the use of harder drugs. In one such study completed in 2006, researchers at the University of Pittsburgh spent 12 years tracking a group of subjects from adolescence into adulthood and documented their initiation into and progression of drug use. The researchers found that a person's likelihood of transitioning to hard drugs is not determined by use of a preceding drug, such as marijuana, but instead by the user's individual tendencies and environmental circumstances.

> "Drugs such as heroin, amphetamines, cocaine, alcohol, and nicotine cause the brain to produce increased amounts of dopamine."

"The idea that marijuana is a 'gateway' drug has been once again squelched by a scientific study," writes Bruce Mirken, an opinion writer for the *Sacramento News and Review*. "This should be the final nail in the coffin of the lie that has propelled some of this nation's most misguided policies: the claim that smoking marijuana somehow causes people to use hard drugs, often called the 'gateway theory.'"[18]

Method of Drug Intake

Drugs can be injected, smoked, snorted through the nose, or swallowed, but the risk of addiction is greatest with drugs that are injected and smoked. Drugs that are smoked or injected enter the brain within seconds, immediately producing a powerful high, or rush of pleasure. The high typically fades quickly, within minutes, and then leaves the user feeling very low, or abnormally depressed. Scientists believe that this low feeling drives individuals to repeated drug use in an attempt to feel better and regain the high. As this cycle continues, the risk of becoming addicted rises.

According to the Mentor Foundation, an organization dedicated to reducing cocaine abuse, smoking results in a more intense high than snorting, but the high does not last as long. "The faster the absorption, the more intense the high. On the other hand, the faster the absorption, the shorter the duration of action. The high from snorting may last 15 to 30 minutes, while that from smoking may last 5 to 10 minutes."[19] Injecting also produces a shorter, more intense, high. For this reason, those who smoke or inject drugs will feel the need to take drugs again sooner than those who take the same drugs by other means. Increasing the number of times they use drugs adds to the risk of addiction.

Emotional Addiction

Some professionals believe that behind every drug addiction there is an underlying emotional trauma that has remained unresolved and unexplored. According to psychologist Morteza Khaleghi, who has treated people with addiction and emotional problems for more than 25 years, emotional trauma can be caused by events such as losing a loved one, the breakup of a significant relationship, and physical or sexual abuse.

Professionals like Khaleghi believe that people will take drugs to the point of addiction because they cannot handle the painful feelings inside them, and the drugs mask the pain. "I know that addiction and emotional issues go hand and hand because I see it in living color every day of my life,"[20] writes Khaleghi. According to Khaleghi, addiction can only be cured if the emotional issues are dealt with through therapy.

Because emotional trauma has begun to be recognized as a common cause of addiction, there are treatment centers that deal specifically with emotional trauma and addiction. For example, the Orchid is an alcohol and drug treatment center in Palm Springs, Florida, that describes itself as specifically for women suffering from addiction and unresolved trauma stemming from physical, sexual, and emotional abuse. The Orchid professionals help the women understand and deal with their trauma while treating their addiction. "The consequences of untreated trauma in early sobriety can be severe," states the Orchid's Web

> " The risk of addiction is greatest with drugs that are injected and smoked. "

site. "Without the protective numbing of alcohol or drugs, newly sober women are often forced to confront painful feelings for the first time in years."[21] Treatment centers such as this one offer specific services and programs to help patients recognize and recover from trauma so that they can more effectively beat their addictions.

Mental State

A person's mental state also affects the likelihood of developing an addiction. A Duke University Medical Center study involving 20,291 individuals found that more than half of those who were diagnosed as drug abusers and addicts also suffered from one or more mental disorders (such as depression or being bipolar) at some point during their lifetime. In the study sample, 50 percent of marijuana abusers and 76 percent of those who abused cocaine also had experienced some type of mental disorder. The state of having both mental illness and addiction is termed "dual diagnosis."

> "The state of having both mental illness and addiction is termed 'dual diagnosis.'"

Mental illness is thought to make a person more prone to self-medicating, which can then lead to addiction. "In an attempt to get relief from the symptoms of the disorder, a drug would be used," writes Lura Seavey, who has worked in the substance abuse field for many years. "For example, if a man suffered from severe depression, he might find temporary relief in the euphoric effects of alcohol. Conversely, if a woman with bipolar [disorder] were experiencing a manic high, she might seek out a sedating drug such as marijuana or even heroin to ease the severity of her symptoms."[22]

Risks to Teenagers

Although taking drugs at any age can lead to addiction, research shows that the earlier a person starts using drugs, the more likely it is that he or she will go on to become a drug abuser or addict. This is because a young person's brain is still developing, particularly the part of the brain that controls reasoning and decision making.

A Yale University study found that adolescent brains reinforce new experiences, such as taking drugs, in stronger ways than do the brains of adults. The reason this happens is that the areas of a teenager's brain that control impulsive behavior are not fully formed, but the brain circuits that reinforce drug use are. This means that teenagers' brains will tell them to use drugs again and that they lack the control to stop from acting on this message.

Although teenagers have the added risk of becoming addicted to drugs when experimenting, no one is exempt. There are many variables that determine whether a person is likely to become addicted when he or she tries a substance like alcohol or drugs. Some people may be able to use these substances recreationally their entire lives without risk of addiction, but others, due to their genetics, environment, and emotional state, may become addicted to any substance they try.

Primary Source Quotes*

What Causes Drug Addiction?

66 One very common belief is that drug abusers should be able to just stop taking drugs if they are only willing to change their behavior. What people often underestimate is the complexity of drug addiction—that it is a disease that impacts the brain and because of that, stopping drug abuse is not simply a matter of willpower. 99

—National Institute on Drug Abuse, "Understanding Drug Abuse and Addiction," July 27, 2009. www.nida.nih.gov.

The National Institute on Drug Abuse is part of the U.S. government's National Institutes of Health, with a mission to use science to understand and fight drug abuse and addiction.

66 Characterizing addiction as a brain disease misappropriates language more properly used to describe conditions such as multiple sclerosis or schizophrenia—afflictions that are neither brought on by sufferers themselves nor modifiable by their desire to be well. 99

—Sally Satel and Scott Lilienfeld, "Addiction Isn't a Brain Disease, Congress," *Slate*, July 25, 2007. www.slate.com.

Satel is a staff psychiatrist at Oasis Clinic in Washington, D.C., and Lilienfeld is a professor of psychology at Emory University.

Bracketed quotes indicate conflicting positions.

* Editor's Note: While the definition of a primary source can be narrowly or broadly defined, for the purposes of Compact Research, a primary source consists of: 1) results of original research presented by an organization or researcher; 2) eyewitness accounts of events, personal experience, or work experience; 3) first-person editorials offering pundits' opinions; 4) government officials presenting political plans and/or policies; 5) representatives of organizations presenting testimony or policy.

❝Of course, not everyone becomes an addict. That's because we have other, more analytical regions [of the brain] that can evaluate consequences and override mere pleasure seeking.❞

—Michael Lemonick, "How We Get Addicted," *Time*, July 5, 2007. www.time.com.

Lemonick is a science writer who has written for publications such as *Science Journalist* and *Time*.

❝Emotional trauma is at the heart of addiction but once the addiction is formed, the physical dependence acquires a life of its own.❞

—Morteza Khaleghi, *Free from Addiction: Facing Yourself and Embracing Recovery*. Hampshire, England: Palgrave Macmillan, 2008.

Khaleghi has treated addicts for more than 25 years.

❝Addiction of all types—to nicotine, alcohol and drugs—is often found in people with a wide variety of mental illnesses, including anxiety disorders, unipolar and bipolar depression, schizophrenia, and borderline and other personality disorders.❞

—American Psychological Association, "Mental Illness and Drug Addiction May Co-occur Due to Disturbance in Brain's Seat of Anxiety and Fear," December 2, 2007. www.apa.org.

The American Psychological Association is a scientific and professional organization that represents psychologists in the United States.

❝Between the ages of 18 and 22, I was homeless and I began using drugs and alcohol. It started out that I would use occasionally but it quickly progressed. I noticed that when I would use, I would feel nothing. It felt good to be numb and I wanted this feeling every day.❞

—Hope, "Hope's Story," Lund Family Center, 2008. www.lundfamilycenter.org.

Hope was addicted for years before she finally became clean and is now on the staff of Lund Family Center, a treatment center that she attended.

❝My fears would grow inside me until they permeated my entire being. Once I got into drugs, I felt less fear.❞

—Karen Franklin and Laura King, *Addicted Like Me*. Berkeley, CA: Seal, 2008.

Franklin and King are mother and daughter who both have struggled with addiction and who wrote a memoir together.

❝Parents who fight regularly—or have recently separated or divorced can cause young people to escape into drug and alcohol use. Some will take drugs to self-medicate their pain, while others will do it as an act of rebellion against the parents who are causing them stress.❞

—Newport Academy, "Most Common Reasons Kids Start Using Drugs," 2009. www.newport-academy.com.

The Newport Academy is a residential drug treatment program for teenagers.

❝Keep in mind that plenty of people go through family deaths, divorce, and other problems and do not abuse drugs. They find other ways to manage their pain and don't create an addiction.❞

—Erica Krull, "A Parent's Fear," Psych Central, July 2009. http://blogs.psychcentral.com.

Krull is a practicing licensed mental health counselor in Nebraska.

❝As the brain develops, we move into adulthood. If the brain is not allowed to fully develop, or that development is slowed because of teenage drug abuse, you can see that the child is in serious jeopardy of having problems.❞

—Drug Addiction Support, "Teenage Drug Abuse," 2009. www.drug-addiction-support.org.

Drug Addiction Support is an online resource for parents and teenagers to learn more about drugs, the problems they can cause, drug addiction, and how to treat it.

Facts and Illustrations

What Causes Drug Addiction?

- According to a 2006 Florida State University study, boys who had very low self-esteem in the sixth or seventh grade were **1.6 times more likely** than other children to meet the criteria for drug dependence nine years later.

- The 2007 National Comorbidity Survey found that **52 percent** of people diagnosed with PTSD are also alcohol abusers or alcohol dependent, which is twice as many as the general adult population.

- **Thirty-five percent** of people with PTSD are also drug abusers or drug dependent, which is nearly three times as many as the general adult population, reports the 2007 National Comorbidity Survey.

- Genetics, mental health, and environment are all factors that determine if the person will be one of the **10 percent** who experiment with drugs and go on to become addicted, according to the University of Utah's Genetic Science Learning Center.

- Alcoholism among individuals with a family history of this addiction is about **four to eight times more common** than in individuals with no such family history, according to a 2006 study in *Alcoholism: Clinical and Experimental Research*.

- Researchers at the Yale School of Medicine have identified a **gene** that makes a person more likely to develop a dependence on drugs such as heroin, morphine, and OxyContin.

Causes of Addiction

Anyone can become addicted to drugs. However, some people are more likely to become addicted than others. This chart shows various risk factors, both biological and environmental, that can increase a person's chance of becoming addicted.

Risk Factors

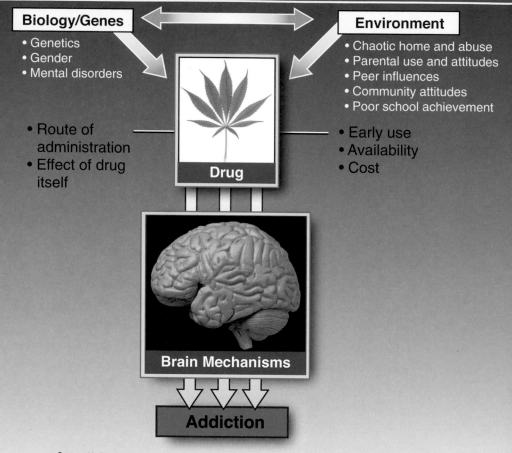

Biology/Genes
- Genetics
- Gender
- Mental disorders

- Route of administration
- Effect of drug itself

Environment
- Chaotic home and abuse
- Parental use and attitudes
- Peer influences
- Community attitudes
- Poor school achievement

- Early use
- Availability
- Cost

Drug

Brain Mechanisms

Addiction

Source: National Institute on Drug Abuse, "The Science of Addiction," February 2008. www.nida.nih.gov.

- In 2008 the National Institute on Drug Abuse reported that studies of **identical twins** indicate that as much as half of an individual's risk of becoming addicted to nicotine, alcohol, or other drugs depends on his or her genes.

Mental Disorders Increase Risk of Substance Abuse and Addiction

Scientific studies have shown that people with a mental illness are more likely than others to abuse drugs, which can lead to addiction. A National Institute of Mental Health study found that antisocial personality disorder and episodes of manic behavior carry higher risk for substance abuse and addiction than illnesses such as phobia or obsessive-compulsive disorder.

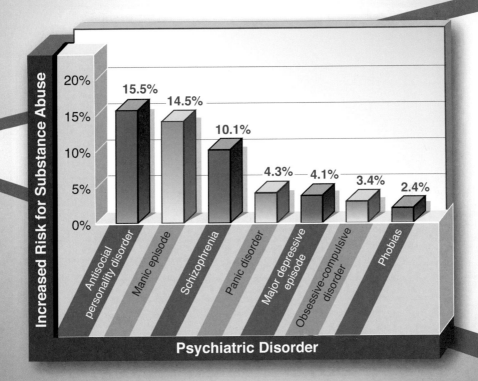

Source: Mental Health America, "Factsheet: Dual Diagnosis," www.nmha.org.

- In 2008 scientists in China identified about **400 genes** that appear to make some people more easily addicted to drugs.

- In 2007 Nora D. Volkow, director of the National Institute on Drug Abuse, reported that all addictive drugs increase the level of **dopamine** in the brain, reinforcing a person's cravings for drugs.

Increased Dopamine Fuels Addiction

In the brain, dopamine is released in response to pleasurable or satisfying activities such as eating. The release of dopamine causes the person to want to repeat the activity. Studies have found that some drugs increase the amount of dopamine released in the brain, causing drug users to want to take drugs again and again. The following diagram shows the amount of dopamine released in the brain when a person eats a meal and when a person uses cocaine.

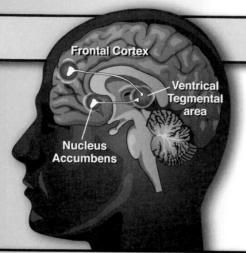

Brain reward (dopamine) pathways

These brain circuits are important for natural rewards such as food, music, and art.

All drugs of abuse increase dopamine

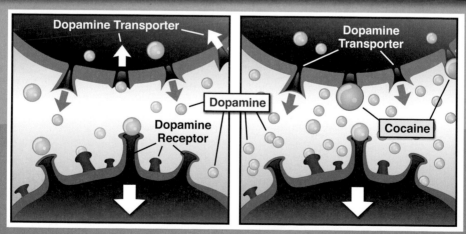

Typically, dopamine increases in response to natural rewards such as food. When cocaine is taken, dopamine increases are exaggerated, and communication is altered.

Source: National Institute on Drug Abuse, "All Drugs of Abuse Target the Brain's Pleasure Center," www.drugabuse.gov.

What Are the Dangers of Drug Addiction?

66Addiction is a disease and like any disease, tears away at the mind and body of the sufferer.99

—Spencer Recovery Centers, a group of recovery centers that have been treating people suffering from marijuana addiction for more than 15 years.

66I was living in a storage shed, going through my second divorce and losing custody of the youngest of my three kids. I was facing felony charges yet again— surely this time I was going to prison.99

—Tom Cramer, recovering methamphetamine addict.

Physical Harms

Drug addiction causes physical problems in users because all drugs, if excessively used, can cause some type of physical harm. Certain drugs, such as nicotine, alcohol, and cocaine, produce more severe and long-term physical damage than other drugs. People addicted to these drugs can harm their health to the point that even if they stop using, the damage cannot be repaired.

Addicted smokers are at risk for extensive damage to their lungs, resulting in problems with breathing. Chronic smoking is a major cause of emphysema and bronchitis, both diseases that make it difficult for people to breathe. Additionally, excessive smoking contributes to a person's chances of cancer. According to the American Cancer Society, cigarette smoking accounts for at least 30 percent of all cancer deaths and is a major cause of cancers of the lung, larynx (voice box), oral cavity, pharynx (throat), and esophagus.

Alcoholics also are at risk because alcohol damages the transmission of nerve impulses in the brain and nervous system. As a result, alcoholics may end up experiencing loss of balance, numbness of the feet and hands, and tremors. Also, according to the American Liver Foundation, up to 35 percent of heavy drinkers develop alcoholic hepatitis, a condition that can lead to progressive and permanent liver damage.

> " **Addicted smokers are at risk for extensive damage to their lungs.** "

Cocaine is another substance that can cause severe and irreversible physical damage to a person; addicts increase their risk of physical harm from this drug because of the frequency of their cocaine use. For example, in the first hour after taking a hit of cocaine, a person's risk of heart attack increases nearly 24 times. Because cocaine addicts are chronic users of the drug, they have a sevenfold lifetime risk of heart attack compared with nonusers. Aside from heart attacks, cocaine addicts increase their risk of respiratory failure, strokes, and seizures, and because cocaine typically decreases a person's appetite, chronic users can become malnourished.

Increased Overdose Risk

One of the most dangerous aspects of being an addict is the increased chance of a drug overdose. An overdose is when a person takes too much of a certain drug and the body cannot process it sufficiently, resulting in normal body functions failing. People who become addicted to drugs have a greater chance of experiencing an overdose than nonaddicts, because addicts have developed a high tolerance to their drugs. In order to achieve a high, addicts must take more and more of the drug, elevating their chances of experiencing a drug overdose. In 2009 the Centers for Disease Control and Prevention released its report on the causes of death in the United States for the year 2006. The report stated that 39,000 of the deaths were due to drug-induced causes, and about 90 percent of those drug fatalities were due to sudden death from overdose.

Few drug addicts who overdose are lucky enough to survive and get a second chance at life. Jonathan Mead is one of the fortunate few. Mead started smoking cigarettes as a teenager, then moved on to marijuana, alcohol, and eventually cocaine. He became so addicted to cocaine that he would lose track of how many hits of cocaine he took in a day. One night he decided to swallow all the cocaine he had left, even though he had already taken some cocaine earlier in the day. "My heart was racing, my body was shaking and I was having heart palpitations," Mead remembers. "The intensity had become too much. I decided I was going to go upstairs to our loft to lay down and try to relax. The last thing I remember was telling my girlfriend that I loved her."[23] Mead woke up to find he had overdosed and was being rushed to the hospital. The doctors were able to save him; this traumatic event made Mead realize how addicted he was, and as a result he got treatment and has remained drug-free since the overdose.

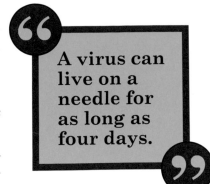

A virus can live on a needle for as long as four days.

The Danger of Needles

Most addicts are so determined to achieve their high from drugs that they not only disregard the dangers of the drugs themselves but also the tools they use to get high. Injecting drug addicts often share needles because many times sterile syringes are not readily available, and addicts are more concerned with getting high then being careful about the needles they use. In 2008 the National Survey on Drug Use and Health found that 13 percent of injection drug users had used a needle that they knew or suspected someone else had used before them the last time they injected. Additionally, less than one-third of them cleaned the needle with bleach before using it.

Using dirty needles puts addicts at risk for numerous diseases because a contaminated needle is an efficient transmitter of blood-borne diseases. A virus can live on a needle for as long as four days. Sharing needles brings the danger of transmitting HIV, hepatitis C, hepatitis B, hepatitis A, and other viral diseases; of these, HIV and hepatitis C and B can be fatal. According to the National Institute on Drug Abuse, approximately one-third of AIDS cases and half of all new hepatitis C cases in the United States result from injection drug use. Addicts who inject put themselves at great risk of contracting these diseases.

Dangers to Newborns

Pregnant drug addicts risk not only their own lives but also the health of their babies. Drugs can cross through the mother's placenta to the fetus and cause major physical damage and even death. Babies born to mothers with a heroin addiction usually have to receive treatment for withdrawal symptoms that include hyperactivity, convulsions, diarrhea, fever, sleep abnormalities, and respiratory distress. The baby of a methamphetamine addict can be born with addiction to methamphetamine and experience tremors, sleep problems, mental and physical disabilities, and decreased motor coordination later in life.

According to the March of Dimes, the more a pregnant woman smokes, the greater her risk of having a low-birth-weight baby. Low-birth-weight babies have increased risk of serious health problems such as respiratory distress syndrome and bleeding in the brain during the newborn period and can develop lifelong problems such as high blood pressure and diabetes. Nicotine addicts who continue smoking during pregnancy nearly double their risk of having a low-birth-weight baby. A 2008 report in *Pediatrics* found that women who smoke any time from the month before pregnancy to the end of the first trimester are more likely to have a baby with birth defects, particularly congenital heart defects. According to the March of Dimes, currently at least 10 percent of women in the United States smoke during pregnancy, putting their babies at risk for birth defects.

> " Fetal alcohol syndrome results in mild to severe physical, mental, behavioral, and/or learning disabilities. "

Alcoholism in pregnant women can lead to fetal alcohol syndrome, a condition that affects 1 in 100 newborns each year. Fetal alcohol syndrome results in mild to severe physical, mental, behavioral, and/or learning disabilities with possible lifelong implications. According to the National Organization for Fetal Alcohol Syndrome, over 125,000 newborns every year are exposed to heavy or binge drinking while in the womb, which is common among alcoholics, and these newborns are at the highest risk for being born with fetal alcohol syndrome.

Ruined Lives

Drug addiction can ruin a person's personal life because addicts put drugs or alcohol at the center of their lives, and as a result they are at higher risk of losing their jobs, going into debt, and destroying relationships with family and friends. Divorce is one of the more common personal problems that occur among substance addicts. In their book *Divorce: Causes and Consequences*, authors Alison Clarke-Stewart and Cornelia Brentano report that the divorce or separation rate among alcoholics is at least four times that of the general population.

In addition to damaging relationships between husbands and wives, drug addiction can harm people's relationships with their children. Charlotte Sanders's drug addiction ended up harming her relationships with her daughters in addition to getting her in trouble with the law. She was in her twenties and the mother of two little girls when she became addicted to methamphetamine. As much as she loved her daughters, drugs became the center of her life, and she would do anything to get them. "I got sneaky and very greedy. I kept running out of money and dope, so I started pawning stuff out of my house, and taking my kids' piggy bank money that grandparents and people had given them,"[24] Sanders writes. Over the years Sanders was arrested and often put herself in dangerous situations but could not break her habit. She looks back at her life with regret and sadness.

> "Drug addicts are more likely to end up in jail than nonaddicts."

Addicts not only ruin their own lives, but they also harm those around them. According to a 2007 report from the Department of Health and Human Services, over 8.3 million children in the United States live with at least one parent who is dependent on or abuses alcohol or illicit drugs. "In families where alcohol or other drugs are being abused, behavior is frequently unpredictable and communication is unclear," states the Children of Alcoholics Foundation, a center that helps children and adults from addicted families. "Family life is characterized by chaos and unpredictability. Behavior can range from loving to withdrawn to crazy."[25] According to the Substance Abuse and Mental Health Services Administration (SAMHSA), research shows that children of parents who abuse drugs are more at risk than their peers for delinquency, depression, poor school performance, and alcohol and drug use.

Addiction and Crime

Drug addicts are more likely to end up in jail than nonaddicts because many buy and use illegal drugs. Arrest is even more likely for addicts who sell drugs to pay for their habit. Each year, according to the U.S. Department of Justice, 1.8 million people are arrested for drug violations of these types.

Eric Stone is an example of an addict who ended up in jail due to his addiction. By his twenties, methamphetamine had become the most important part of Stone's life. His mother kicked him out of the house for stealing from her, but Stone kept sneaking back to hide items he had stolen and planned to sell later to pay for his drug habit. Stone writes:

> On one particular occasion I tried to sneak in my house when my mom caught me and called the police. I quickly hid behind some bushes in the neighbor's yard waiting for the police to leave so I could try to sneak in again. As I watched the house I noticed one of the officers carrying out some stereo equipment that I had recently stolen. I knew right away I was in big trouble. I soon had a new home: the county jail.[26]

It was during his jail time that Stone started his recovery, and though he relapsed two times following his initial recovery, he has since turned his life around.

Special Dangers for Drug-Addicted Teens

According to the Partnership for a Drug-Free America, 1.4 million American teens have substance abuse problems, including abuse and addiction. These teenagers put themselves at risk for all of the typical dangers associated with drug addiction. They also risk their long-term health in ways that do not affect adults, specifically in terms of brain development.

The prefrontal cortex of the brain is not fully mature in a teenager. This part of the brain allows people to understand situations and make sound decisions while keeping emotions and desires under control. Using large amounts of drugs while this part of the brain is still developing may have long-lasting consequences. "A young person may recover quickly from a single or occasional use of a drug, but repeated use may result in brain changes that are long lasting,"[27] writes Don Vereen, special assistant to the director of the National Institute on Drug Abuse.

Teenage addicts endanger their brains, their physical health, and their chances at living normal lives. They, and addicts of all ages, cannot live healthy, fulfilling lives unless they confront their addiction and work toward sobriety. If they do not, they put themselves at increased risk for unemployment, jail time, divorce, sickness, and even death.

Primary Source Quotes*

What Are the Dangers of Drug Addiction?

66 Alcohol controlled my life for seven years. I was on a path of self destruction. It nearly cost me my wife and children, and I now realize it might have eventually cost me my life. 99

—Andrew Smith, "Alcohol Can Change Your Life," 388th Fighter Wing, October 4, 2007. www.388fw.acc.af.mil.

Smith is a recovering alcoholic serving in the U.S. Air Force.

....

66 When I was 19 years old, I was smoking up to 30 cigarettes a day at University, and with a night out, it could easily reach 40 a day. I switched to a stronger brand, yet still smoked more and was in constant pain. A University doctor told me I had the lungs of a 40-year-old smoker and I wasn't even 20. 99

—James, "Conquering Nicotine Addiction—a Teen Smoker's Story," About.com, January 22, 2008. http://quitsmoking.about.com.

James became addicted to cigarettes at age 15 and was able to finally quit at age 21.

....

* Editor's Note: While the definition of a primary source can be narrowly or broadly defined, for the purposes of Compact Research, a primary source consists of: 1) results of original research presented by an organization or researcher; 2) eyewitness accounts of events, personal experience, or work experience; 3) first-person editorials offering pundits' opinions; 4) government officials presenting political plans and/or policies; 5) representatives of organizations presenting testimony or policy.

" People who are addicted to a drug are more likely to get an infectious disease such as HIV, either through unsafe sex or by sharing needles. "

—Mayo Clinic, "Complications," October 2, 2009. www.mayoclinic.com.

The Mayo Clinic is a not-for-profit medical practice dedicated to the diagnosis and treatment of virtually every type of complex illness.

....

" I had been on drugs since I was thirteen and at twenty gave birth to a beautiful baby boy. He was hooked on cocaine, though, and that was totally my fault. They put him in neonatal intensive care and then told me he would be going to a foster home. I would be going to jail. "

—Amber, "Amber's Story," Narconon, October 21, 2009. http://addiction.narcononrehab.com.

Amber has been in recovery for more than six years and has since regained custody of her son.

....

" Women with addictive disorders who receive Temporary Assistance for Needy Families are significantly more impaired than those without such disorders. They have more physical and mental health problems and are less likely to have graduated from high school or have labor market skills. "

—National Center on Addiction and Substance Abuse at Columbia University, "Intensive Case Management for Substance-Dependent Women Receiving Temporary Assistance for Needy Families," January 2009. www.casacolumbia.org.

The National Center on Addiction Substance Abuse at Columbia University is a nonprofit organization that works to educate Americans about the economic and social costs of substance abuse and addiction.

....

❝I found myself alone with nowhere to sleep, or eat, and I was out in the cold. I thought to myself 'Oh my God! I'm homeless!' It was like someone had hit me upside the head. I'd lost all of my friends, I'd lost the life I once had, all I had was my drugs.❞

—Anonymous, "Another Day, Another Dose, Part 2," Narconon, October 19, 2009. http://addiction.narcononrehab.com.

The author is a recovered OxyContin addict who went through the Narconon program.

....

❝Many drug abusers end up in prison or jail. Sometimes they steal property to get money for drugs. Or, often they will commit crimes while 'high' on drugs.❞

—National Institute on Drug Abuse, "Treating Drug Addiction: What Offenders and Families Need to Know," May 5, 2009. www.drugabuse.gov.

The National Institute on Drug Abuse is part of the U.S. government's National Institutes of Health, with a mission to use science to understand and fight drug abuse and addiction.

....

❝More than any other age group adolescents are at risk for substance addiction, and more than any other age group they risk permanent intellectual and emotional damage due to the effects of drugs.❞

—Science and Management of Addictions Foundation, "The Effects of Drugs and Alcohol on the Adolescent Brain," 2008. www.samafoundation.org.

Science and Management of Addictions Foundation is a nonprofit organization with the goal of improving the management and science of substance addiction.

....

Facts and Illustrations

What Are the Dangers of Drug Addiction?

- According to the American Liver Foundation, between **10 and 20 percent** of heavy drinkers develop cirrhosis, severe liver scarring, which is not reversible and is a life-threatening disease.

- A 2009 National Center on Addiction and Substance Abuse report stated that substance abuse and addiction constitutes the United States' number 1 public health problem, contributing to more than **70 health conditions** and to the **5 leading causes of death**.

- The American Cancer Society reports that habitual smoking is responsible for almost **9 out of 10** lung cancer deaths.

- In a 2009 report the Centers for Disease Control and Prevention states that more than **35,000** people in the United States died from drug overdoses in 2006.

- According to the National Organization on Fetal Alcohol Syndrome, fetal alcohol syndrome caused by a woman's excessive alcohol drinking during pregnancy affects **1 in 100 infants** each year.

- A University of Chicago study reveals that the number of pregnant women seeking treatment for methamphetamine addiction, which can **harm the fetus during pregnancy,** tripled between 1994 and 2006.

Drug Abuse Violations on the Rise

The following chart shows by year the increasing number of arrests for drug abuse violations in the United States from 1982 to 2007. These violations include the unlawful possession, sale, use, growing, and making of narcotic drugs, marijuana, synthetic narcotics, and nonnarcotic drugs such as barbiturates.

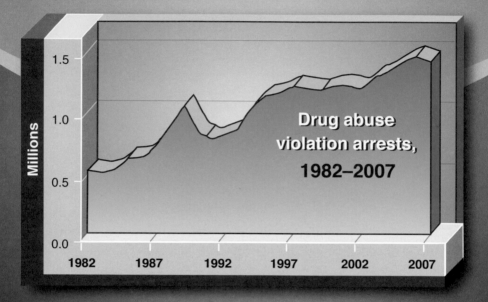

Drug abuse violation arrests, 1982–2007

Source: Bureau of Justice Statistics, "Risk Factors," August 17, 2009. www.ojp.gov.

- **7.3 million children** in the United States lived with a parent who was dependent on or abused alcohol, and about **2.1 million** lived with a parent who was dependent on or abused illicit drugs in the past year, according to a 2007 SAMHSA report.

- According to a 2008 SAMHSA report, more than three-quarters **(77 percent)** of the American public believe that an individual with an addiction to illicit drugs such as heroin, cocaine, or methamphetamine is a **danger to society**.

Substance Addiction Threatens Society

In 2008 the U.S. Substance Abuse and Mental Health Services Administration (SAMHSA) surveyed Americans to determine their perceptions of the dangers posed by substance addiction. More than 75 percent of the American public believe that an individual with an addiction to illicit drugs such as heroin, cocaine, or methamphetamine poses a danger to society. Only one-third of Americans perceive marijuana addiction as a danger, and respondents are almost evenly split on the issue of alcohol addiction. The survey also found that women more often see substance addiction as a threat to society than men.

How much do you agree or disagree that a person with an addiction to the following substances is a danger to society?

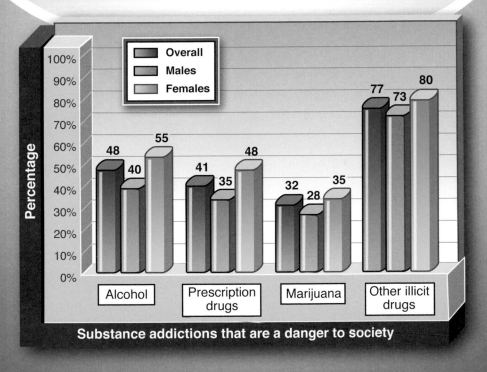

Source: SAMHSA, "Survey for SAMHSA on Addiction and Recovery," September 2008. www.samhsa.gov.

- According to SAMHSA, children growing up with parents who are addicted to alcohol or illegal drugs are **four times more likely** to become drug abusers themselves.

Methamphetamine Addiction Among Pregnant Women Rises

An increasing number of pregnant women may be endangering their babies because of their addiction to methamphetamine. Babies exposed to methamphetamine during pregnancy may develop long-term developmental problems. A University of Chicago study found that in 1994 methamphetamine use accounted for 8 percent of all substance addiction treatment center admissions for pregnant women, but by 2006 that number had risen to 24 percent.

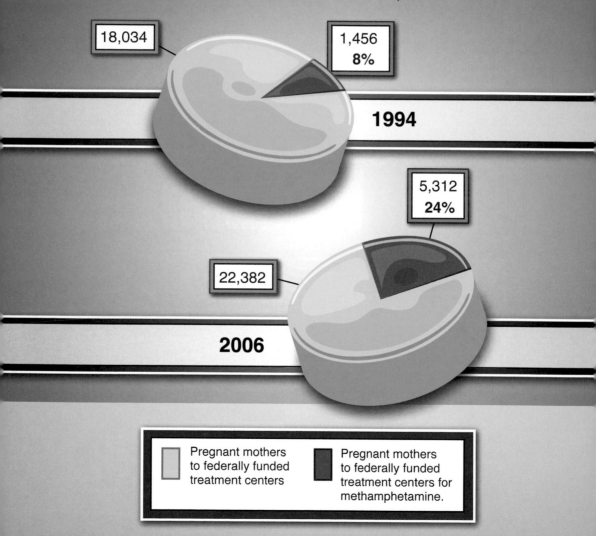

18,034

1,456
8%

1994

5,312
24%

22,382

2006

Pregnant mothers to federally funded treatment centers

Pregnant mothers to federally funded treatment centers for methamphetamine.

Note: Numbers taken only from federally funded treatment centers.

Source: Serena Gordon, MedicineNet, "Methamphetamine Use Triples Among Pregnant Rehab Patients," May 21, 2009. www.medicinenet.com.

Can Drug Addiction Be Overcome?

66Like many diseases, addictions may also be managed but not always cured.99

—Mark Cowell, director of Charleston County, S.C., Department of Alcohol and Other Drug Services.

66If you don't pull it together for yourself, no one else will. That's coming from a person who had to try it all . . . and who still loves to have a good time.99

—Drew Barrymore, actress, discussing her drug and alcohol addiction.

Admitting Addiction

Recovery from addiction depends first and foremost on the addict admitting that he or she has a problem. Sometimes this occurs when family members confront the addict. However, most of the time addicts only acknowledge their drug use as a problem after a traumatic event such as an arrest or injury.

Brett Carlson had been abusing drugs for many years before he realized how out of control his drug problem was. He said:

> I had a lot of LSD in my system and things went really
> bad. I thought I had died and gone to hell. I saw the devil.
> I ended up running through the city streets to my friend's

home. My friend's parents called my parents and they took me to the hospital and put [me] in a psych ward. My parents were petrified. I was petrified. It was the first real sign that my life was on the line. Directly after that experience, I went into my first outpatient rehab.[28]

It was that experience that set Carlson on his road to treatment and recovery.

Detoxification Comes First

Nearly all drug addiction treatment programs begin with detoxification, which is when the addict completely stops using drugs and allows his or her body to rid itself of all drugs. This can be an extremely difficult time because the addict is mentally and physically dealing with withdrawal, the cravings and pain the body feels because it lacks the drugs or alcohol it has become accustomed to.

During withdrawal, addicts can experience a variety of emotional symptoms, including depression and sleeplessness and actual physical problems ranging from shakiness to hallucinations. Robert Keney, a methamphetamine addict, woke up one day and decided he could no longer stand his addicted life, so he entered a rehabilitation facility for detoxification. "I will never forget how bad it felt to come down. I felt bugs crawling out of my skin. I was sweating, and I was in so much pain,"[29] Keney said. Despite the pain Keney endured the withdrawal and went on to recover from his addiction.

Many Choices

According to the National Survey on Drug Use and Health, 4 million persons aged 12 or older received treatment for drug addiction or alcohol abuse in 2008. Many of these people got treatment at on-site or off-site centers that provided counseling, behavioral therapy, psychotherapy, medication, case management, and other services. The majority of addicts who got treatment attended no-cost facilitated self-help groups such as Alcoholics Anonymous, one of the best-known treatment programs for alcoholics. At these meetings recovering addicts learn to follow 12 steps to maintain sobriety, are paired with a sponsor who has been in recovery for a longer period, and provide encouragement and advice to one another.

The effectiveness of treatment programs varies. Narcotics Anonymous, which is similar to Alcoholics Anonymous, works with people who are addicted to narcotics. According to a 2007 survey of over 13,000 of its members, the average length of time members had maintained abstinence from drugs was 9.1 years. As for treatment centers, different centers report different numbers of successes. Follow-up surveys done in 2008 for the Saint Jude Retreat House, a drug rehabilitation treatment center in New York, found that between 51 and 63.7 percent of those who attended Saint Jude and responded to the survey remained sober after completing the 6-week program.

> " Most of the time addicts only acknowledge their drug use as a problem after a traumatic event. "

Inability to Afford Treatment

Although there are many drug and alcohol treatment centers available, the cost of participation in some of them can be very high. The average cost for inpatient programs is $7,000 per month, reports the National Survey of Substance Abuse Treatment Services. According to the 2008 National Survey on Drug Use and Health, 32.1 percent of people who believed they needed drug addiction treatment did not get it because they could not afford it.

The U.S. government has instituted a program to help those who want treatment for addiction but cannot afford it. Begun in 2004, Access to Recovery provides vouchers to addicts in financial need. They can use these vouchers to get substance abuse treatment and recovery support services. By 2007, $300 million in funds were awarded, and more than 170,000 people with substance abuse problems received treatment through the program.

Special Programs for Teenagers

In 2008, according to the SAMSHA National Survey on Drug Use and Health, 1.9 million youths in the United States aged 12 to 17 were in need of treatment for a drug or alcohol problem. As the number of teenagers who need treatment has increased, the number of treatment facilities specially geared to young adults has risen as well. "Unlike their adult counterparts, adolescents in treatment have more family difficulties, are more likely to have psychological problems, and are more likely to have attempted suicide," states the Drug Rehab Treatment Web site of CRC Health Group, a provider of treatment and educational programs for adults and youth. "Their alcohol and drug-use patterns are also differ-ent. Teens tend to abuse multiple substances, while adults are more singular in their focus."[30]

> **During withdrawal, addicts can experi-ence a variety of emotional symptoms, including depression and sleeplessness.**

Another difference between adults and teens entering treat-ment is that for most teens, re-ferral to treatment is involuntary; teens who seek treatment often go because parents, school, or a judge has required them to do so. This means that the treatment facilities also have to focus on getting their young clients to understand that they have a problem and need help. "Many of our clients are here be-cause their parents required them to attend," said Heather Schnoebelen, the clinical manager at Four Circles, a treatment center for youth. "They may spend their first week or two struggling with the realization that they have a problem, but by the time they leave our care, they not only admit that they have a problem but are motivated to continue to change."[31]

Chance of Relapse

No matter what form of treatment a drug addict gets, there is a high chance that he or she will relapse. According to the National Institute on Drug Abuse, drug addiction relapse rates range from 40 to 60 percent.

Many professionals say that relapse does not mean the recovering addict has failed. Treatment of addiction involves changing embedded behaviors, and such changes can take several tries. "Relapse should not be viewed as a failure; it is part of a learning process that eventually leads to recovery,"[32] says Susan Merle Gordon, author of *Relapse & Recovery: Behavioral Strategies for Change*.

Kelly Osbourne, daughter of rock star Ozzy Osbourne, is an example of a recovering drug addict who relapsed several times before she felt she was truly recovered. She became addicted to Vicodin by the time she was 17 and eventually admitted she had a problem, spending 30 days at a drug treatment center. However, she relapsed and later admitted she was not ready to beat her addiction. She ended up going to three different rehabilitation centers and in 2009 said that her last visit finally made her realize she had a serious problem. "After 30 days, I left rehab. For the first time, I felt hopeful," said Osbourne of her last treatment. "I knew I'd been given another chance at my life, at my career, at happiness. I wanted to grab it."[33]

Medicated Treatment

Because certain drugs—particularly alcohol, cocaine, and opiates such as heroin—are so physically addictive, efforts to stop taking them usually lead to major withdrawal symptoms and/or severe cravings. Certain prescribed drugs that are carefully monitored by doctors can help the drug addict deal with these symptoms and cravings, increasing the addict's chances at recovery.

One of the most common medications prescribed for addicts undergoing heroin withdrawal is methadone, which is a synthetic opiate that blocks the effects of heroin and eliminates withdrawal symptoms. There are over 10,000 methadone treatment centers in the United States that prescribe and monitor methadone for use by heroin addicts. However, methadone itself is addictive, and some heroin addicts end up addicted to methadone. In October 2002 the Food and Drug Administration approved buprenorphine, another drug that can also be used to help heroin addicts during withdrawal. Buprenorphine results in a lower level of physical dependence, so patients who discontinue the medication generally have fewer withdrawal symptoms than those who stop taking methadone.

> " Teens who seek treatment often go because parents, school, or a judge has required them to do so. "

When alcoholics go through withdrawal, they often experience major cravings that cause many to fail in their recovery. A common drug used to help an alcoholic abstain from alcohol is Antabuse, which makes addicts vomit and experience headaches if they drink alcohol. A newer drug for alcoholic treatment is naltrexone, which reduces relapse rates and cravings. One study found that use of naltrexone resulted in 38 percent of patients relapsing to alcohol dependence, versus the 60 percent relapse rate among those who took the placebo.

New Ways to Reduce Cravings

Researchers are also looking for a drug to help cocaine addicts deal with withdrawal and cravings. Currently, researchers have found that taking prescribed amphetamines, specifically dexamphetamine, may help cocaine addicts stop using cocaine, because using dexamphetamine cancels out the desired high a user would normally get from the cocaine. One British study tracked 60 stimulant addicts who were treated with dexamphetamine and found that about two-thirds of patients stopped using over a 10-month period.

Scientists are also trying to reduce drug cravings by enhancing the brain's neurotransmitter gamma-aminobutyric acid (GABA). Drug use increases dopamine production, which in turn increases an addict's drug cravings. GABA lowers the level of dopamine, resulting in a decrease of cravings. Researchers have developed a prescription drug called baclofen, which, after ingested, binds to the GABA receptor in the brain and then prevents the release of dopamine. In 2007 researchers from the Institute of Internal Medicine, Catholic University of Rome published a study that showed the effectiveness of baclofen for treating alcoholic cravings. In the study of 42 alcohol-dependent patients who took baclofen, 30 of them achieved and maintained abstinence, compared with 12 of the 42 patients who took a placebo. A 2009 trial of 60 smokers found that those who took baclofen were able to reduce their smoking from 20.5 cigarettes a day to 8, compared with the placebo group, which cut down to 12 cigarettes.

> " The vaccines being developed are designed to reduce or eliminate the amount of addictive substance that reaches the user's brain. "

Vaccines for Addicts

One of the latest areas of research into addiction treatment is the development of vaccines to help reduce drug cravings in those addicted or who are recovering from substance addiction. The vaccines being developed are designed to reduce or eliminate the amount of addictive substance that reaches the user's brain, which then eliminates the high a person gets from drugs. Without the desired high, the user's craving for drugs is reduced.

One vaccine known as TA-CD (therapy for addiction—cocaine addiction) is being developed by Thomas Kosten, a psychiatry professor, and his wife, Therese Kosten, a neuroscientist and psychologist, at Baylor University College of Medicine in Texas. TA-CD is designed for people struggling to overcome addiction or to avoid relapse. In 2009 the Kostens released the results of Phase I of the vaccine study, which so far has shown positive results.

Another vaccine under development is NicVAX, which is designed to help addicts stop smoking and to prevent relapses. NicVAX gets the immune system to produce antibodies that bind to nicotine, which prevents the nicotine from entering the brain and producing a high, thereby reducing a person's desire to smoke. In 2009 Nabi Biopharmaceuticals announced that it had begun the first of two Phase III clinical trials for NicVAX, and results are anticipated in 2011.

Although scientists have great hope for medical ways to help fight addiction, most agree that stopping addiction still requires behavioral changes. Addicts must want to stop using and be willing to work to change their habits and ingrained behavior. However, once addicts are ready to stop taking drugs or alcohol, these scientific developments, along with all of the other behavioral and medical treatments already available, can help them achieve and maintain a drug-free lifestyle.

Can Drug Addiction Be Overcome?

66 **Many addicts are ashamed of their addiction and are afraid to make it public. Others are still in denial that they have a problem. Still others are uneducated about programs available to them, or think they can't afford treatment.** 99

—Bethany Winkel, "September Is National Alcohol and Drug Addiction Recovery Month," Treatment Solutions Network, September 4, 2009. www.treatmentsolutionsnetwork.com.

Winkel is a frequent writer on various drug addiction topics for the Treatment Solutions Network, an organization that helps addicts find treatment centers and provides educational information about drug addiction and treatment.

66 **The majority of all treatment programs offer a group recovery approach as the primary or secondary component of their treatment modality. Unfortunately, these groups are often counterproductive to overcoming addiction and leave the individual at risk for continued relapse.** 99

—David Roppo, "Overcoming Addiction," Five Steps to Addiction Freedom, 2007. www.5stepstoaddictionfreedom.com.

Roppo is an addiction coach who has authored books about addiction and how to treat it.

Bracketed quotes indicate conflicting positions.

* Editor's Note: While the definition of a primary source can be narrowly or broadly defined, for the purposes of Compact Research, a primary source consists of: 1) results of original research presented by an organization or researcher; 2) eyewitness accounts of events, personal experience, or work experience; 3) first-person editorials offering pundits' opinions; 4) government officials presenting political plans and/or policies; 5) representatives of organizations presenting testimony or policy.

66 Drug interventions are a positive and supportive way of allowing friends and family to express their concerns for a loved-one. Involving a professional interventionist is a good idea because he or she can teach the members of the group what to expect from the person suffering from a drug addiction and how to deal with it. 99

—Recovery Connection, "Drug Addictions," 2007. www.recoveryconnection.org.

The Recovery Connection is a private referral network that helps people find drug addiction treatment within the continental United States.

66 Few people have the strength to go it alone, and when the pains get bad and pills can be bought at the nearest pharmacy, it's hard to maintain resolve. For the best chance at sobriety you need professional help. 99

—Choose Help, "Detox," 2009. www.choosehelp.com.

Choose Help is an organization dedicated to helping addicts find an appropriate treatment program.

66 Very few rehabilitation programs have the evidence to show that they are effective. The resort-and-spa private clinics generally do not allow outside researchers to verify their published success rates. The publicly supported programs spend their scarce resources on patient care, not costly studies. 99

—Benedict Carey, "The Evidence Gap," *New York Times*, December 28, 2008.

Carey is an American journalist who writes about medical and science topics.

66 There are no quick fixes for any chronic illness including addiction, which is why patients deserve sympathy and support, even when they relapse. 99

—Harold C. Urschel III, "Addiction Is a Chronic Brain Disease," Intervene, September 25, 2009. http://intervene.drugfree.org.

Urschel is the chief medical strategist at EnterHealth LLC.

❝Without effective treatment, abuse of alcohol, illicit drugs, or prescription medications can devastate the mind and body. With treatment, substance use disorders can be managed, giving individuals the effective tools necessary to address their addiction.❞

—Barack Obama, White House, August 31, 2009. www.whitehouse.gov.

Obama is the forty-fourth president of the United States.

❝Those [women at the treatment center] taught me how to live. They showed me how to walk, talk, be a lady, cut out all the old behaviors, narrow down all the boyfriends, be a mother.❞

—LaChele Young, "Drugs Don't Discriminate," Partnership for a Drug-Free America, 2009. www.drugfree.org.

Young was a cocaine addict until she suffered a heart attack at the age of 29. She then turned her life around, first staying in a hospital and then getting treatment at Safe Haven.

❝Essentially, Methadone maintenance therapy allows recovering opiate addicts to function without the pains of withdrawal or a craving for the drug of abuse, and since they are not 'high' while using Methadone, they are able to participate meaningfully in society, and are far less likely to return to abuse, crime and other risky behaviors.❞

—Choose Help, "Methadone Drug Rehab," 2009. www.choosehelp.com.

Choose Help is an organization dedicated to helping addicts find an appropriate treatment program.

❝Despite methadone clinics' best efforts, if you give drugs to addicts, they will find a way to abuse them. . . . The addiction community has known this for decades, but it's something that drug replacement therapy seems to ignore.❞

—Tyler Francke, "Methadone Not the Answer for Eastern Maine's Addicts," *Maine Campus*, September 24, 2009. http://mainecampus.com.

Francke writes editorials for the University of Maine paper, the *Maine Campus*.

Can Drug Addiction Be Overcome?

- The National Survey on Drug Use and Health reports that in 2008, **4 million** persons aged 12 or older received treatment for an addiction or abuse of alcohol or illicit drugs.

- According to Drug Rehab, an organization dedicated to helping addicts find treatment, the most extreme symptoms of alcohol withdrawal involve **delirium tremens**, a potentially fatal condition experienced by about **5 percent** of recovering alcoholics.

- Narcotics Anonymous has over **33,500 meetings per week** in 115 countries.

- According to a 2008 *New York Times* article, every year, state and federal governments spend more than **$15 billion**, and insurers at least **$5 billion** more, on substance abuse treatment services for some **4 million** people.

- The National Institute on Drug Abuse reports that for every dollar spent on addiction treatment programs, there is an estimated **four- to seven-dollar reduction** in the cost of drug-related crimes.

- The National Institute on Drug Abuse reports that the average cost for one full year of methadone maintenance treatment is approximately **$4,700 per patient**.

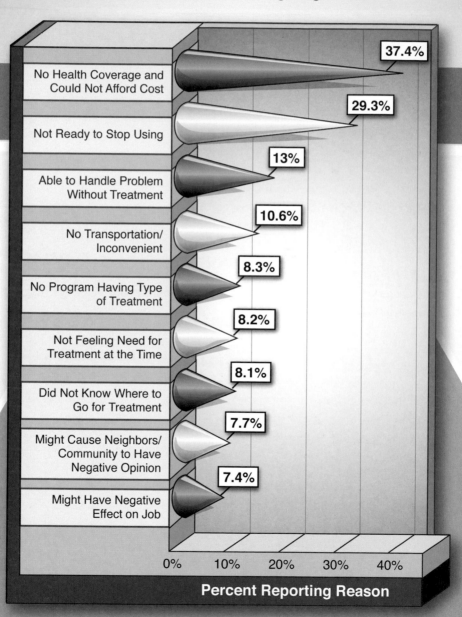

Why Addicts Do Not Get Treatment

According to the 2008 National Survey on Drug Use and Health, over 20 million people aged 12 and older in the United States needed but did not get treatment for drug and alcohol abuse. The chart lists the reasons given for not getting treatment.

Reason	Percent
No Health Coverage and Could Not Afford Cost	37.4%
Not Ready to Stop Using	29.3%
Able to Handle Problem Without Treatment	13%
No Transportation/Inconvenient	10.6%
No Program Having Type of Treatment	8.3%
Not Feeling Need for Treatment at the Time	8.2%
Did Not Know Where to Go for Treatment	8.1%
Might Cause Neighbors/Community to Have Negative Opinion	7.7%
Might Have Negative Effect on Job	7.4%

Percent Reporting Reason

0% 10% 20% 30% 40%

Source: National Survey on Drug Use and Health, "National Findings," 2008. www.oas.samhsa.gov.

American Public Supports Addiction Treatment

A majority of Americans believe that health care reform should include making alcohol and drug addiction treatment more accessible and more affordable, according to a 2009 survey sponsored by the Open Society Institute.

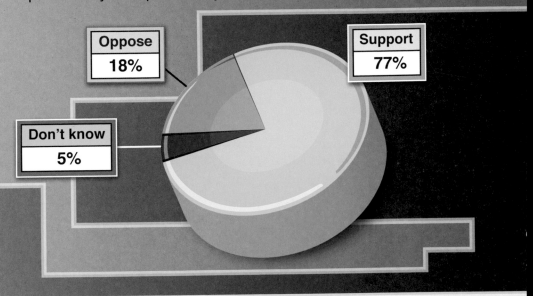

Oppose 18%

Support 77%

Don't know 5%

The survey also found that support for improving access to more affordable addiction treatment spans political party affiliation.

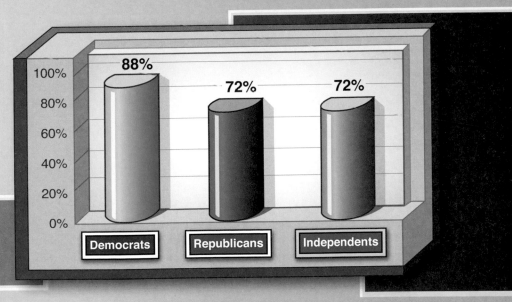

Source: Open Society Institute, "Poll: Open Society Institute/Lake Research Partners," September 2009. www.soros.gov.

Substance Abuse Treatment Choices

The following chart shows the different drug addiction programs people in the United States attended in 2008. The most popular were self-help programs, with nearly 2.2 million Americans attending them.

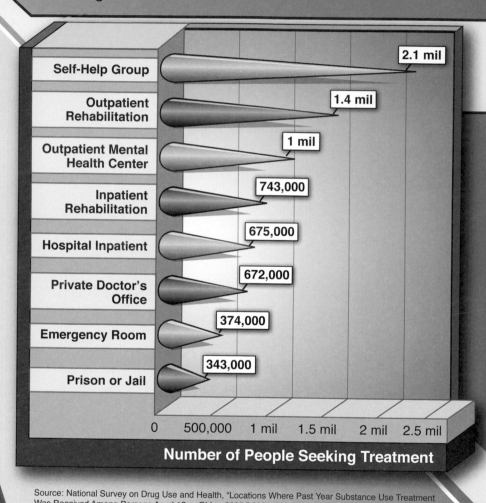

Self-Help Group — 2.1 mil

Outpatient Rehabilitation — 1.4 mil

Outpatient Mental Health Center — 1 mil

Inpatient Rehabilitation — 743,000

Hospital Inpatient — 675,000

Private Doctor's Office — 672,000

Emergency Room — 374,000

Prison or Jail — 343,000

0   500,000   1 mil   1.5 mil   2 mil   2.5 mil

Number of People Seeking Treatment

Source: National Survey on Drug Use and Health, "Locations Where Past Year Substance Use Treatment Was Received Among Persons Aged 12 or Older: 2008," 2008. http://oas.samhsa.gov.

- According to the 2008 National Survey on Drug Use and Health, over **20 million** people aged 12 and older in the United States needed, but did not receive, treatment at a facility for illicit drug or alcohol abuse and addiction.

- The Substance Abuse and Mental Health Services Administration reports that as of September 2008, Access to Recovery, a U.S. program dedicated to helping people who cannot afford to get drug addiction treatment, has delivered treatment or recovery support services to more than **260,000 people in need.**

- A 2009 survey by the National Center on Addiction and Substance Abuse at Columbia University found that **49 percent** of people surveyed said they would not be able to afford alcohol or drug treatment if they or someone in their family needed it.

- More than three-quarters of all Americans, including 72 percent of Republicans, 88 percent of Democrats, and 72 percent of Independents, support including **addiction treatment in health care reform,** according to a poll released by the Closing the Addiction Treatment Gap initiative in 2009.

- A University of California at Los Angeles study of **1,167 adolescents** receiving substance abuse treatment found that those in treatment for 90 days or more had significantly lower relapse rates than those in programs of 21 days.

- According to the National Institute on Drug Abuse, drug addiction relapse rates range from **40 to 60 percent.**

Key People and Advocacy Groups

Alcoholics Anonymous: This nonprofit organization was established in 1935 and today has over 2 million members. Its purpose is to provide alcoholics a free way to recover through meetings that follow its 12-step program.

Betty Ford: Ford is the wife of former U.S president Gerald Ford. She battled chemical dependency and was open about this with the public, encouraging others to admit and get treated for their own addictions. In 1982 she cofounded the nonprofit Betty Ford Center in Rancho Mirage, California, which treats both men and women with chemical addictions.

R. Gil Kerlikowske: Kerlikowske is the director of the U.S. Office of National Drug Control Policy. He establishes policies, priorities, and objectives for the nation's drug control program.

Narcotics Anonymous (NA): This organization is a nonprofit group dedicated to providing a recovery process and peer support network to drug addicts around the world. The 12 steps are the principles NA members follow during their group meetings. In 2007 there were over 25,065 groups holding over 43,900 weekly meetings in 127 countries.

National Institute on Alcohol Abuse and Alcoholism: This government organization is part of the U.S. National Institutes of Health. It leads national efforts to reduce alcohol-related problems through research, training, and working with international, national, state, and local institutions.

National Institute on Drug Abuse: This government organization is part of the U.S. National Institutes of Health. It leads national efforts to use science to fight drug abuse and addiction.

Drew Pinksy: Pinksy is the medical director for the Department of Chemical Dependency Services at Las Encinas Hospital in Pasadena, California. He has become well known for overseeing the rehabilitation of celebrity addicts.

Betty Tai: Tai is the director of the Center for Clinical Trials Network of the National Institute on Drug Abuse. Tai leads the efforts of research projects that study behavioral, pharmacological, and integrated treatment interventions and determines the effectiveness of these treatments.

Nora D. Volkow: Volkow became the director of the National Institute on Drug Abuse (NIDA) at the National Institutes of Health in 2003. As leader of the NIDA, she runs programs that research the health aspects of drug abuse and addiction.

Chronology

3500 B.C.
This is the earliest year for which the production of alcohol is recorded. An ancient Egyptian papyrus describes a brewery.

1935
Bob Smith and Bill Wilson found Alcoholics Anonymous.

A.D. 1493
Columbus and his crew introduce the use of tobacco to Europe. The indigenous people in the Americas introduced him to its use.

1914
The U.S. Congress passes the Harrison Narcotic Act, which forbids the sale of substantial doses of opiates or cocaine except by licensed doctors and pharmacies.

1500   1800   1900   1915   1930

1844
Cocaine is isolated in its pure form.

1937
Cannabis is made illegal in the United States with the passage of the Marihuana Tax Act.

1875
Opium dens, which became popular in California during the early 1800s, are outlawed in San Francisco.

1919
The Eighteenth Amendment to the U.S. Constitution, which prohibits the manufacture, sale, and importation of intoxicating liquors, is ratified on January 16, 1919.

1938
LSD, also known as acid, is first synthesized on November 16, 1938, by Swiss chemist Albert Hofmann.

1940s
During World War II, amphetamines are widely distributed to U.S. soldiers to combat fatigue and improve both mood and endurance.

2009
U.S. president Barack Obama proclaims September 2009 as National Alcohol and Drug Addiction Recovery Month.

1993
The nicotine patch is developed and sold as an over-the-counter method to help people stop smoking.

1967
The "summer of love" in San Francisco links drugs to the counterculture movement with the philosophy of "sex, drugs, and rock and roll."

1982
Cocaine usage peaks in the United States with 10.4 million users.

1940   1960   1980   2000

1948
Wyeth pharmaceutical company begins to sell Antabuse, the first medicine approved for the treatment of alcohol abuse and alcohol dependence by the U.S. Food and Drug Administration.

1988
The White House Office of National Drug Control Policy, a component of the Executive Office of the President, is established by the Anti-Drug Abuse Act.

2008
An estimated 22.2 million persons aged 12 or older in the United States abuse or are dependent on substances.

1970
The Controlled Substances Act is passed by Congress and establishes rules for methadone clinics that provide methadone to heroin addicts who are trying to stop their heroin use.

Related Organizations

American Association for the Treatment of Opioid Dependence Inc.

225 Varick St., 4th Floor

New York, NY 10014

phone: (212) 566-5555 • fax: (212) 366-4647

e-mail: info@aatod.org • Web site: www.aatod.org

This organization was founded in 1984 to enhance the quality of patient care for people dependent on opioids. It does so by promoting the growth and development of methadone treatment services throughout the United States. The organization provides educational materials, conferences, and studies regarding opioids and methadone treatment.

American Lung Association

490 Concordia Ave.

St. Paul, MN 55103

phone: (651) 227-8014 • fax: (651) 227-5459

e-mail: mhavell@lungusa.org • Web site: www.lungusa.org

The American Lung Association's mission is to improve lung health and prevent lung disease. The association has many programs to fight lung disease, including a variety of smoking control and prevention programs targeted to specific groups such as nicotine addicts. Its Web site provides information about smoking, its dangers, and ways to stop.

American Medical Association (AMA)

515 N. State St.

Chicago, IL 60654

phone: (800) 621-8335

Web site: www.ama-assn.org

The mission of the AMA, founded in 1847, is to better public health through the science of medicine. The AMA does this by advocating for certain health care–related legislation and providing publications and other materials to physicians regarding a variety of medical issues, including substance abuse and addiction.

American Society of Addiction Medicine

4601 N. Park Ave., Upper Arcade #101

Chevy Chase, MD 20815

phone: (301) 656-3920 • fax: (301) 656 3815

e-mail: email@asam.org • Web site: www.asam.org

This organization's mission is to improve the quality of addiction treatment, provide to physicians the latest information about addiction medicine, and make addiction medicine a specialty recognized by medical and government organizations. The organization produces several publications about the latest news in addiction medicine.

Betty Ford Center

PO Box 1560

Rancho Mirage, CA 92270

phone: (760) 773-4100 • fax: (760) 674-8853

e-mail: admissions@bettyfordcenter.org

Web site: www.bettyfordcenter.org

The Betty Ford Center is an addiction treatment center with the mission to help men and women who want to break their addictions. The center is a licensed addiction hospital that has treated nearly 60,000 patients in the past 20 years.

Hazelden Foundation

15245 Pleasant Valley Rd.

Center City, MN 55012

phone: (651) 213-4200 • fax: (651) 213-4536

e-mail: info@hazelden.org • Web site: www.hazelden.org

Hazelden is a national nonprofit organization founded in 1949 with the mission to help people reclaim their lives from addiction. A nationally respected treatment center with several clinics, Hazelden provides treatment and continuing care for youths and adults.

National Youth Anti-Drug Media Campaign

PO Box 6000

Rockville, MD 20849-6000

phone: (800) 666-3332 • fax: (301) 519-5212

e-mail: www.whitehousedrugpolicy.gov/utilities/contact_form.html

Web site: www.whitehousedrugpolicy.gov/mediacampaign

The National Youth Anti-Drug Media Campaign, created in 1988, is a program of the Office of National Drug Control Policy. This campaign's goal is to teach teens to stand up to the pressure to use drugs and alcohol.

Partnership for a Drug-Free America

405 Lexington Ave., Suite 1601

New York, NY 10174

phone: (212) 922-1560 • fax: (212) 922-1570

e-mail: www.drugfree.org/Portal/Contact/ • Web site: www.drugfree.org

The Partnership for a Drug-Free America is a nonprofit organization that brings together parents, scientists, and communications professionals to help families raise drug-free children. The partnership helps parents prevent their children from using drugs and alcohol by providing parents with information and training tools that they can use.

Substance Abuse and Mental Health Services Administration (SAMHSA)

PO Box 2345

Rockville, MD 20847-2345

phone: (877) 726-4727 • fax: (240) 221-4292

e-mail: shin@samhsa.hhs.gov • Web Site: www.samhsa.gov

This administration works to help people who are in need of recovery or are at risk for mental or substance abuse disorders. SAMHSA provides publications about the latest drug addiction and treatment information. It also provides grants for research into substance abuse and mental disorder studies.

White House Office of National Drug Control Policy (ONDCP)

PO Box 6000

Rockville, MD 20849-6000

phone: (800) 666-3332 • fax: (301) 519-5212

e-mail: www.whitehousedrugpolicy.gov/utilities/contact.html

Web site: www.whitehousedrugpolicy.gov

The ONDCP is part of the Executive Office of the President and was established by the Anti-Drug Abuse Act of 1988. The main goals of ONDCP are to establish policies, priorities, and objectives for the nation's drug control program.

For Further Research

Books

Marina Barnard and Fergal Keane, *Drug Addiction and Families*. London: Jessica Kingsley, 2007.

Kelly Barth, *The History of Drug Abuse*. Detroit: Greenhaven, 2007.

Rod Colvin, *Overcoming Prescription Drug Addiction: A Guide to Coping and Understanding*. Omaha, NE: Addicus, 2008.

John Hoffman and Susan Froemke, *Addiction: Why Can't They Just Stop?* Emmaus, PA: Rodale, 2007.

Charles Rubin, *Don't Let Your Kids Kill You: A Guide for Parents of Drug and Alcohol Addicted Children*. Petaluma, CA: New Century, 2008.

David Sheff, *Beautiful Boy*. New York: Houghton Mifflin, 2008.

Nic Sheff, *Tweak: Growing Up on Methamphetamines*. New York: Atheneum, 2007.

Periodicals

John Cloud, "Can One Drug Addiction Cure Another?" *Time*, March 8, 2009.

Economist, "How to Stop the Drug Wars," March 5, 2009.

———, "One Success in the Drug Wars," May 1, 2008.

———, "Treatment on a Plate," October 16, 2008.

Claudia Kalb, "And Now, Back in the Real World," *Newsweek*, March 3, 2008.

New York Times Upfront, "The Truth About 'Rehab' & Drug Addiction: The Reality Is Far from Glamorous," April 6, 2009.

Anthony Papa, "Drug Addiction Is an Illness, Not a Crime," *Albany (NY) Times Union*, July 8, 2008.

Maia Szalavitz, "Can Amphetamines Help Cure Cocaine Addiction?" *Time*, December 8, 2008.

———, "Treating Alcohol Addiction: A Pill Instead of Abstinence?" *Time*, July 29, 2009.

Isabel Tiotonio, "The Last Day of Rehab; We Follow Five Women Who Completed an Intensive Drug-Addiction Program. Their Odds of Success Are Not Great," *Toronto Star*, July 4, 2009.

Nora Volkow, "The Truth About 'Rehab' and Drug Addiction," *Science World*, April 6, 2009.

Yorkshire Post (UK), "Winehouse Fights Drug Addiction in Rehab," January 25, 2008.

Internet Sources

Mayo Clinic, "Drug Addiction," October 2, 2009. www.mayoclinic. com/health/drug-addiction/DS00183.

National Institute on Drug Abuse, "Drug Abusing Offenders Not Getting Treatment They Need in Criminal Justice System," January 13, 2009. www.nida.nih.gov/newsroom/09/NR1-13.html.

———, "Monitoring the Future Survey: Overview of 2008 Results," April 2, 2009. www.nida.nih.gov/newsroom/08/MTF08Overview. html.

White House Office of National Drug Control Policy, "Teens and Drug Use: Parents' Rx for Prevention," 2009. www.theantidrug.com/ advice/expert-advice/general-parenting/dr-drew-chat.aspx.

———, "Treatment Programs," 2009. www.whitehousedrugpolicy.gov/ treat/treatment_programs.html.

Source Notes

Overview

1. Michael Reichman, "I Looked Like a Dead Person," Partnership for a Drug-Free America, June 2, 2006. www.drugfree.org.
2. Quoted in San Francisco Gate, "Reynolds Vows to Inspire Addicts," September 18, 2009. www.sfgate.com.
3. National Institute on Drug Abuse, "Drug Abuse and Addiction," September 17, 2008. www.drugabuse.gov.
4. Janet Firshein, "Introduction: Addiction as a Disease." Web Companion piece to Moyers on Addiction: Close to Home, PBS. www.pbs.org.
5. Sally Satel and Scott Lilienfeld, "Addiction Isn't a Brain Disease, Congress," *Slate*, July 25, 2007. www.slate.com.
6. Quoted in Corrections Connection, "Drug Abusing Offenders Not Getting the Treatment They Need in the Criminal Justice System," July 20, 2009. www.corrections.com.
7. Patrick Meninga, "How to Stay Clean and Sober After Leaving Rehab," Spiritual River, October 2, 2007. www.spiritualriver.com.

What Is Drug Addiction?

8. Mindy McConnell, "I Could Never Get High Enough," Partnership for a Drug-Free America, May 9, 2006. www.drugfree.org.
9. Quoted in Sarah Kershaw and Rebecca Cathcart, "Marijuana Is a Gateway Drug for Two Debates," *New York Times*, July 17, 2009. www.nytimes.com.
10. Mayo Clinic, "Prescription Drug Abuse," June 28, 2008. www.mayoclinic.com.

11. Dawn, "Patient Stories," National Alliance of Advocates for Buprenorphine Treatment. www.naabt.org.
12. Sarah Senghas, "Cross Addiction: An Addiction to Drugs, No Matter What Kind," Associated Content, April 15, 2008. www.associatedcontent.com.
13. Quoted in Richie Salgado, "Drug Dependency, a Disease Not a Crime," Philstar, March 2, 2009. www.philstar.com.
14. Quoted in Addiction Info, "Can an Alcoholic Have an Occasional Drink?" November 12, 2008. www.addictioninfo.org.

What Causes Drug Addiction?

15. Quoted in *Know Your World Extra*, "Free Again: This Teen Is Fighting Drug Addiction—and Getting His Life Back," November 3, 2006, p. 6.
16. Quoted in *Science Daily*, "PTSD Can Lead to a More Severe Course and Worse Outcomes for a Substance-Abuse Disorder," March 4, 2008. www.sciencedaily.com.
17. Quoted in University of Utah, "Genetics Is an Important Factor in Addiction," December 12, 2008. http://learn.genetics.utah.edu.
18. Bruce Mirken, "Not a Gateway, Dammit," Marijuana Policy Project, August 23, 2007. www.mpp.org.
19. The Mentor Foundation, "Cocaine," September 2, 2009. www.mentorfoundation.org.
20. Morteza Khaleghi, *Free from Addiction: Facing Yourself and Embracing Recovery*. Hampshire, England: Palgrave Macmillan, 2008, p. 4.
21. Orchid Recovery Center, "Individualized Addiction Treatment," 2009.

www.orchidrecoverycenter.com.

22. Lura Seavey, "Dually Diagnosed," Suite 101.com, September 19, 2006. http://substanceabuse.suite101.com.

What Are the Dangers of Drug Addiction?

23. Jonathan Mead, "A Light in the Dark," Illuminated Mind, 2008. www.illuminatedmind.net.

24. Charlotte Sanders, "I Felt Like Super Mom," Partnership for a Drug-Free America, June 5, 2006. www.drugfree.org.

25. Children of Alcoholics Foundation, "Effects of Parental Substance Abuse on Children and Families." www.coaf.org.

26. Eric Stone, "The Meth Trap," Partnership for a Drug-Free America, August 24, 2005. www.drugfree.org.

27. Don Vereen, "Research Shows the Consequences of Drug Abuse on the Teenage Brain," *Challenge*. www.eric.ed.gov.

Can Drug Addiction Be Overcome?

28. Brett Carlson, "In the Palm of My Right Hand," Partnership for a Drug-Free America, 2009. www.drugfree.org.

29. Robert Keney, "Breaking the Cycle," Partnership for a Drug-Free America, 2009. www.drugfree.org.

30. Drug Rehab Treatment, "Treating Teens for Substance Abuse," 2003. www.drugrehabtreatment.com.

31. Quoted in Meghan Vivo, "My Child Refuses to Enter a Substance Abuse Treatment Program: What Can I Do?" Drug Rehab Treatment. www.drugrehabtreatment.com.

32. Quoted in Kathie Keeler, "Does Relapse Mean Treatment Failure?" Take Good Care of Yourself, March 24, 2009. www.tgcoy.com.

33. Quoted in Exposay, "Kelly Osbourne Became Addicted to Vicodin by the Time She Was 17," August 28, 2009. www.exposay.com.

List of Illustrations

List of Illustrations

Index

About the Author

Leanne K. Currie-McGhee lives in Norfolk, Virginia, with her husband, Keith, and two beautiful girls, Hope and Grace. She has been writing educational books for several years.